An Evangelical
Faith
for Today

John Lawson

Abingdon Press
Nashville • New York

AN EVANGELICAL FAITH FOR TODAY

Copyright © 1972 by Abingdon Press

ISBN 0-687-12180-9

Library of Congress Catalog Card Number: 75-186826

MANUFACTURED BY THE PARTHENON PRESS, AT
NASHVILLE, TENNESSEE, UNITED STATES OF AMERICA

And he said unto me, Son of man, go, get thee unto the house of Israel, and speak with my words unto them. . . . As an adamant harder than flint have I made thy forehead: fear them not, neither be dismayed at their looks, though they be a rebellious house. . . . Nevertheless if thou warn the righteous man, that the righteous sin not, and he doth not sin, he shall surely live, because he is warned; also thou hast delivered thy soul.—Ezekiel 3:4, 9, 21

Contents

1 God and the World

It is a matter of general knowledge, which no impartial mind can deny, that there is very widespread grass-roots discontent with much of the theological leadership of the mainline or responsible Christian denominations. It is therefore necessary for someone from a leading representative seminary to address himself candidly to this burning issue. This little book is an attempt to do just this, and to do it constructively.

We all know that resurgent popular evangelical movements take the official leadership of the churches—and particularly the theological leadership of the churches—seriously to task for selling out on the gospel. The conventional answer of defensive Christian academics is to brush this off as ignorant and prejudiced backlash. In bygone years, it is said, Christian education was persecuted by self-appointed and ignorant popular leaders in the churches, who bitterly criticized it for abandoning certain overrigid or naïve positions no thoughtful evangelical maintains nowadays. The seminaries performed a service to the church by insisting on their intellectual integrity and academic independence. And, it is said, the same battle is still being joined.

It must be stated with all possible plainness of speech

that this is simply not the case today. The seminaries are every bit as likely to be in the wrong as are bigoted people in the local congregation. It is common knowledge that some teaching which is regularly, and indeed customarily, given in seminaries is contrary to scripture, and to the chief planks of the historic Christian faith, and to the doctrinal standards of the responsible Christian denominations. We are not here referring to minor doctrinal issues which, in the past, have divided the denominations, such as the pros and cons of predestination, or baptismal regeneration. Nor are we discussing purely speculative issues connected with the doctrine of the Trinity, and the like. We have in mind the leading essential elements of the practical gospel of salvation.

The most painful thing is that seminarians often receive teaching that is diametrically opposed in important particulars to the articles of faith to which they have to subscribe at ordination. They therefore have to choose between disbelieving some of their learned teachers (which many of them fortunately do), or else perjuring themselves on one of the most sacred days of their lives, or refusing to proceed to ordination. And the teaching in question is sometimes given by men who have themselves undertaken these ordination vows! If we are honest men we have to admit that we theological teachers are often in a false and compromised position. Naturally most of the men and women who come to us come from earnest and committed Christian homes and congregations. Many of them, thank God, have had deep experiences of divine call and consecration. And they are not all sheltered youngsters from simple and retired rural homes. They have stood for Christ on unbelieving campuses, in the hard world of business, or in the armed forces. Yet I know from long experience of counseling with them that they often find it a devastating experience to be faced in a seminary with new and ingenious arguments on behalf of unbelief, fortified with an array of scholarship. I have no reason to suppose that the institution where I am proud to serve is any worse in this respect than the average.

Someday there will have to be a great awakening, a far-reaching repentance, and a painful reappraisal. Any institution that wishes to continue as an integral part of the church, committed to the Christian faith and to the training of distinctively Christian ministers and teachers, and which looks to its mother church for sympathy and support, will have to make a definite resolve of priority. This is, that in the selection of both faculty and students the institution will seek as the first and indispensable qualification that a man or woman be a deeply committed Christian disciple, a conscientious upholder of the historic Christian faith, and loving and loyal to the Christian church. Then with this priority satisfied it will seek the ablest scholars it can. However, if it wishes to go the other way, and set itself up to be a purely academic institution committed only to technical scholarship and "know-how," then it must have the courage to say so, and cease to expect the church to regard it with confidence and support as part of herself. Conversely, the church must cease to regard graduation from such an institution as in any sense evidence that a man or woman is qualified for ordination, or to be appointed as a Christian teacher. Everyone will have to be examined from scratch for Christian commitment.

Certainly an academic must have freedom to follow his research where it leads, and to speak the truth as he sees it. However, if his research leads him to call into question the major doctrinal tenets of his church, the only use a morally and intellectually honest man can make of his freedom is to move to a secular institution not committed to the Chris-

tian faith and ministry, there to teach pale, neutral, de-
natured "religion."

"What difference does sound theology make?" some will
ask. "Is not theology simply part of the theory of religion?"
The answer is that the Christian faith is an historic faith.
It is not a set of ideas which various teachers have taken
into their heads, but the message of what God has done.
Therefore, Christian faith cannot be "true for faith but false
in fact." It is sadly possible for a man to be orthodox yet
lacking in vital Christian experience and commitment, and
so, as Wesley put it, "to know as much about saving souls
as catching whales." But it does not work the other way
round! However comforting to faith the Christian message
may seem, it will wither away if there is any suspicion that
it is not in accord with the facts, or right reason. Therefore,
while there have been revivals of Christian devotion that
have been revivals of simpleminded and unreflective en-
thusiasm only, the great and constructive revivals always
have been revivals of sound, balanced, and scriptural theology, as well as of "the heart strangely warmed." The evangelical renewal of the church cannot arise apart from a
renewal of her historic and scriptural evangelical theology.
Hence we make no apology for turning the thoughts of our
readers to what we believe about God.

It is possible for a person to be an atheist in the strict
sense of the word. A resolute and systematic unbeliever can
maintain that the physical universe of matter and force is
all that actually exists, that intelligent mind and spirit are
essentially passing illusions, and that it is not possible to
raise any intelligible question about an originating and overarching rational plan. The universe with all its apparent
order and beauty is a succession of colossal causeless acci-
dents, after the manner of the proverbial chimpanzees strum-

ming on typewriters and writing Shakespeare. The creation is, in fact,

> . . . a tale
> Told by an idiot, full of sound and fury,
> Signifying nothing.

This is the irrational miracle of unbelief accomplished by the obstinate.

Most people who call themselves atheists, however, do not go as far as this. They are not as clear-sighted in their denial of Ultimate Reason. They have decided that they cannot believe in God as he is spoken of in the Bible and in the Christian tradition flowing from the Bible. They regard as a fixed naturalistic evolutionary process the universe of suns and planets, of plant and animal life evolving upon the planet as the environment changes, and of man evolving from organic life, and developing in society, in social mores, in thought and ideals under the pressure of successive ways of making a living. Every stage has happened "inevitably" from what went before. They have little room for the notion of an intelligent creator of the universe, still less for an active governor of the universe who can actually do something in it, and least of all for a loving Father who personally cares for man and will work his blessing.

Yet these reduced believers cannot bring themselves to break entirely with the sentiment of the Christian tradition that lies behind them. A nostalgia for "God-talk" clings to them, the use of which also makes it more comfortable to continue in the church. So they go on speaking about God, but meaning by the word something entirely different from what the Bible means. They mean a general originating and controlling principle—but that is all. No heavenly Person exists to whom a worshiper can intelligibly say his prayers. So if they lead worship they are talking only to the congregation, for there is no one else listening, and, when they pray, they take care not to ask God to do anything, for there is "neither voice, nor any to answer, nor any that regarded" (I Kings 18:29). They sing hymns because it makes them feel good, but they do not seriously believe what they are singing. Their worship is a wave of sentiment, not a confession of faith. We may aptly call these numerous people crypto-atheists. Their practical attitude to life is the same as that of the atheist, though perhaps of a kindly and humane atheist, but their language about that attitude is confused and facing both ways. They are hard to nail down either as atheists or as believers.

It has to be admitted that the dangerous influence in the church is that of the teacher of whom we must say: "The hand is the hand of Esau, but the voice is the voice of Jacob" (Gen. 27:22). He speaks of God, professes sincerely enough to love the ideals of Christ (and so to be a "Christian"), and belongs to the church. Yet he shows himself totally unsure about the actual existence of a personal God, probably doubts whether we know much for certain about Jesus as a divine incarnation, does not believe in the resurrection, does not like the word "atonement" (in fact, assumes that man must save himself by the educational process), does not believe in intercessory prayer, and has no real confidence in any human destiny beyond this present life. This man, who is facing both ways, is likely to mislead the unwary into supposing that he is a teacher of the Christian religion. As Wesley put it, in the title of one of his famous pamphlets, we behold "Christ Stabb'd in the House of His Friends." (Cf. Pss. 41:9 and 55:12-14.)

Now the evangelical (and the Catholic also, of course)

takes up his stand firmly that by the term "God" he means God as He is revealed in the Bible. God is the originating, sovereign, personal King of the creation. He has made the world. He rules it with continuing intelligent control. He can act his wonderful works within it. Man can have personal fellowship with God in prayer and worship, and can reasonably ask God to do things because He is able to answer. This doctrine of God as the personal and active God of religious worship and fellowship is expressed supremely by the biblical phrase the "living God" (Deut. 5:26; Ps. 42:2; Heb. 9:14). We emphatically wipe off the slur so persistently and wrongheadedly cast upon us, that to speak of God as personal means to think of him as having some sort of "body," and existing in some sort of "place."

Christian theology will allow that such phrases as the "Supreme Being," the "Great First Cause," and the "Ground of Being" can rightly be applied to God, for he is all these. Yet every one of them is only partial, and does not by itself sufficiently guarantee the essential biblical element, which is that God is the personal maker and ruler of the world; is separate from, and superior to his handiwork (Ps. 102:25-27; i.e., God is *transcendent*); extends his interested providential care to every detail (Matt. 10:29-31; i.e., God is *immanent*), and summons man to have personal fellowship with Himself in worship, and give Him moral obedience (Isa. 55:6-9).

In the familiar triangulated structure of a bridge the engineer provides a certain number of interdependent main members to carry the load. Every one of them is essential, and, if one breaks, an intolerable strain is placed on the remainder so that the whole collapses. So it is in Christian theology. There are a certain limited number of essential interdependent principles, without any one of which the whole falls down. The first of these is the biblical doctrine of the one personal sovereign God, transcendent and immanent. Without this every other part of Christian belief is indefensible. For example, if God is defined as a remote Absolute, separate from the world, an incarnation becomes a contradiction in terms. If he is defined as a god who cannot perform an action in the world there can be no saving work in the death and resurrection of Christ and, therefore, no gospel of grace.

This salient issue of Christian belief may be illustrated by a brief discussion of the so-called process-theology, a term which is at present popular in many academic theological circles. Anyone who accepts the scientific view of the world in which we live will allow that nature is a *process*. Things happen in a rational order according to fixed laws. The heavenly bodies move in fixed and calculable courses. The environment on the earth seems to change by fixed laws also, though we are less able to calculate them. In response to the environment, organic life of plants and animals adapts itself, and so develops by rational stages. This too is a process. Much of the life of man seems to be a process also. New knowledge produces a new way of earning a living, which produces a new community with hopes and fears and ideals of its own. We do not lightly allow that this is the whole story of human life, but this is a big element in it.

The Christian attitude toward nature is that God started the process in the beginning according to an intelligent and foreseeing plan (Gen. 1:1–2:3; Ps. 33:6-9). As the act of creation took place outside human experience and outside the process, man, by the nature of things, can never understand the divine act. It is an ultimate mystery (Job 38:1-7). Nevertheless, man finds it quite rational to believe in this mystery, because of the inherent difficulty of supposing that the creation, in all its order and wonder, can exist without a sufficient cause.

The Christian also affirms that the process of the world is not a mechanically determined one. The intelligent mind of God can work through its laws and operations to accomplish his good will. This intelligent and beneficent government of the world we call God's Providence (Gen. 45:5; Ps. 124:1-3; Matt. 6:25-33). That it is perfectly rational to believe in the providential government of the world of nature, and divine Providence does not involve breaking the laws of nature, we can judge from experience. When an engineer makes a plane fly through the sky something is happening in the world of nature that would not have happened had not an intelligent mind been at work. Yet the engineer has not "broken" or suspended the invariable law of nature. By understanding it he has worked through it to produce this effect. The only way of affirming that his technical work is part of a law of iron necessity ruling in the process of nature is to maintain that the intelligent mind of the engineer is not really free to think, but is totally conditioned by the material world around him.

If we once allow that the free, intelligent mind of man really exists, the process of nature is not a fixed one. And if the mind of man can operate to a small extent, the all-wise mind of God, with unlimited resources, can do so altogether, and with sovereign effect (Isa. 40:12-31, 43:13). Furthermore, when God's general providential government produces an exceptional wonder, beyond man's expectation and of great spiritual significance, we call it a *miracle* (Luke 7:19-23). Yet we do not rightly regard such a miracle as a breaking of the law of nature, but as a sovereign operation through it. The *process* of nature then—and of human life—is the method by which God has created the world.

When a philosophical theologian describes himself as a process theologian, the validity of his system, from the Christian point of view, entirely depends, as is so often true, upon what he means by the term. If he intends that the world as known to science is a process ruled by natural law, and that an intelligent God is sovereign over it and works his will through it, then we have legitimate Christian philosophical theology. But if he means that God is only the principle of existence of the process, so that there is no room for any saving act of God in human affairs, then his theory cannot be accepted as Christian theology. If the biblical revelation is the determining element in the system, and the idea of process is used to make this revelation intelligible to the modern mind, well and good. But if a naturalistic idea of the universe as a fixed system is the determining element, and the biblical element is reduced in order to accommodate to it, then the system must be rejected by the Christian thinker. The simple test of any such teacher is: Does his system unambiguously allow of a real incarnation of the divine Son, and a real divine action in the world by the Son's life of victory, his death, and real resurrection? If it does not, the system is not to be accepted as legitimate Christian theology.

It may be of interest to some readers at this point to add three notes on more theoretical issues.

Symbolical Language for God

The chief thing to bear in mind is that symbolical language is not vague language, the substitute for exact thought, or the mark that we lack knowledge. Symbolical language is, in fact, the most expressive form of language. We can have matter-of-fact knowledge only of things which can be grasped by the experience of our senses, which can be seen and felt and measured either directly or indirectly by scientific instruments. As soon as the scientist tries to get behind the data he has collected in this way, and to interpret their meaning in a general law, he has to turn to a formula, which is a mental construction, a type of symbol, in fact. The same is true in human personal experience. Matter-of-fact language will suffice for daily business. However, as soon as we are moved imaginatively to powerful emotions and noble aspirations we have to express ourselves in vivid word-pictures, in the language of poetry, in symbolism. This is supremely true of religion, and the things of God.

Men and women have seen visions which have conveyed the sense of the presence of God, but no one has seen or felt or measured God (Deut. 4:11-13, John 1:18). He is not part of our this-worldly experience. So God can be described only in symbolical language; that is to say, in vivid comparisons to things belonging to our this-worldly experience that present conceptions about God to our mind and imagination. Yet this is not a way of admitting that our knowledge of God is vague, insubstantial, or unimportant.

To say God is "the Father" is to draw an imaginative comparison from human affairs. We do not mean that God is a father as a human father is a father, and that he has procreated us. However, a human father is the source of the life of his child; he is the superior of his young child in age and knowledge and power, and so has control of him; and a father is loving, so that he uses his superior status and control unselfishly for the benefit of his child. All this is a picture of God, and of his spiritual relation to us. So by symbolical comparison from human experience God may rightly be expounded as the "Father." So likewise when we declare that God the Father "loves," we do not mean that he loves as humans love, with a physical emotion, for he has no body.

Yet the quality which renders human love spiritually valuable is that the physical attachment can be the means by which one human being treats another as an object of inestimable worth and sacrifices himself for the loved one unselfishly. God has this sort of spiritual attitude toward us: so he loves.

This principle is to be applied to many other of the vivid imaginative metaphors of the Bible. One of the Bible's great texts expressing the idea of the personal God is Exodus 33:11: "And the Lord spake unto Moses face to face, as a man speaketh unto his friend." Moses was granted an experience of communion with God that made the divine presence as real to him as though there were another man standing there. Yet this metaphor does not mean that Moses *saw* anything, or that he thought of God as though He were a kind of man. The beautiful though quaint passage which follows (vv. 12-23) certainly does not involve that the writer thought of God as a big man, with a back as well as a face, and with a hand big enough to cover the mouth of a cave. This is the language of poetry. To try to take it literally is to be most unfair to the spiritual understanding of men of ancient times. It quite unnecessarily makes them seem very childish and primitive.

Nor is dull literalism in any way required as a mark of reverence for the authority of the divine revelation. Symbolical rather than literal language has, by the nature of the case, to be applied to God, and the true question therefore is not whether literal or symbolical interpretation does more justice to scripture, but what sort of symbolism is most illuminating. This judgment requires spiritual sensitivity. A well-intentioned teacher, wishing to avoid the notion that heaven is some sort of "place" above the blue sky, can tell her young children in Sunday school that God is everywhere. The response comes: "Is God in my tummy?" The word "every-where" when applied to God is itself symbolical, and it is a symbol a child cannot understand. It conveys much more truth to them to let them with a good conscience sing, as I did in Sunday school:

> Around the throne of God in heaven
> Thousands of children stand,
> Children whose sins are all forgiven,
> A holy, happy band,
> Singing, "Glory, glory, glory!"

This likewise is symbolical, but more adequately expressive to a child. Yet are we not all children in these matters?

Greek Philosophical Terms in Christian Theology

The proposition that the Christian doctrine of God is based securely upon the Bible and not upon secular philosophies is often challenged by the assertion that the ancient church adopted into its creeds terms from Greek thought. The practical importance of this is that theologians use it as an excuse to move away from the Bible today, though in other directions. Now it is quite correct that the orthodox and authoritative creeds contain such ancient philosophical and therefore nonbiblical phrases as "three divine persons, one divine substance," and the divine Son is "of one substance with the Father." It is very necessary, however, to appreciate the use which the ancient church made of these technical terms.

The problem was how to affirm without any possibility of cavil or evasion that Jesus Christ is divine in the full and proper sense of the word, and also to preserve intact the doctrine that God is one. This was no easy matter. The only intellectual shorthand available were these terms from the secular philosophy of the times. Yet the church used them in order to affirm and to safeguard the original New Testament faith, and to exclude transformation into a hellenistic philosophy. It was the aim of the emasculators of the New Testament Christian faith (the "heretics") to take the presuppositions of Greek philosophy about God and the world into the inward substance of the Christian faith, and, as it were, to change the Christ into a Greek philosophical Christ. This is what the church always rightly resisted. By contrast, orthodox doctrine presents the original New Testament Christ to some extent in a Greek dress, for the purpose of communication. Secular philosophy may be used cautiously as a servant of the divine revelation. It must never be the master. Thus one can have a Christian philosophy in the service of the scriptural faith. Yet Christianity itself is not a philosophy, but a way of devotion, worship, and moral service, based upon an authoritative divine revelation.

The Doctrine of the Trinity

The doctrine of the Holy Trinity is the climax of Christian symbolization for the nature of God. This doctrine has long been the subject of misunderstanding and of obstinate prejudice, on the ground that it is supposed by some to be the perversion of an original "simple" gospel by subtle theological speculators who have rendered the faith difficult by self-contradictory formulae. Actually the doctrine of the Trinity is thoroughly evangelical in derivation, and is to be defended as a proper part of the presentation of the gospel.

The fundamental point is that Jesus Christ is not merely a divine revelation, or the teacher of a divine doctrine which man has to try to follow. He is the performer of a divine saving work in the world of men, and for man. His life, death, and resurrection are an actual divine victory over the guilt and power of sin. This is the element that makes the Christian message into a gospel of grace, and it depends upon the divine nature of our Lord. A great prophet or teacher would suffice to bring a perfect doctrine. Only a divine Lord can be a savior. Yet how can the fundamental doctrine of the one true and living God be expounded in such a way as to safeguard the divinity of Christ? It is this evangelical problem which gave rise to the doctrine of the Trinity as an exposition of New Testament faith.

According to the Bible, God has made himself known to man in three ways. There is the one Creator-God, whom our Lord taught us to call the "Father" (Matt. 6:9), so that the most distinctive Christian title for God is "the God and Father of our Lord Jesus Christ" (Rom. 15:6; Eph. 1:3). In the second place, there is God as he became incarnate, lived for a span of years in Galilee and Jerusalem, taught, died, and rose again. He is described as the divine Son (John 1:18; Heb. 1:1-3). In the third place, there is the Spirit of God, who is also the Spirit of Christ (Rom. 8:9; Gal. 4:6; I Pet. 1:11), the personal agent by whom the activity of the Father and the Son is applied to the lives of men and women in many ages and places.

The question arises: In this three-fold historic experience, has the supreme God really come to us and given us contact with himself? Or is this only an illusion of divine meeting, with God "as he is in himself" still distant, unmoved, unknown, and unknowable? Has God as he is in himself actually made himself known with reliable knowledge, to the limit that man can know God? Or is this only a mere concession to human frailty? The church has always insisted that the answer must be affirmative. God has made himself known in a threefold experience, Father, Son, and Holy Spirit, because from eternity to eternity there is in his nature that which actually corresponds to this. God is admittedly the ultimate mystery, and we do not pretend to know all about him. The infinite is beyond the power of man to grasp. But insofar as man can apprehend a divine revelation, this revelation is the reliable and final word. When we see Him as he is (I John 3:2) in glory we shall know God more fully than we do now (I Cor. 13:12), but we shall also know that God enabled us genuinely and securely to know Him in Christ in this life.

That the Christian doctrine of God should embrace a deep element of mystery is not surprising. The minds of some can stretch further than others, but in every branch of knowledge the intellect even of the ablest comes to the limit of its powers. Existence is a mystery. And God is the principle of that existence. So naturally his being is a mystery, and a "simple" doctrine of God, easy to expound, would be self-condemned as inadequate to the case.

QUESTIONS

1. Does the idea of evolution make it easier or more difficult for you to believe in God as creator?

2. Bishop Robinson in *Honest to God* implied that most conventional Christians have thought about God as though he were "a big man," in a place "above the sky," and indicated almost that the church has been too ready to let them believe this. Do you think this is a fair judgment on what ordinary people think about God?

3. Do you in your own life have any sense of the providence of God, of his guidance, of divine action in remarkable answer to prayer, etc.? Would people be more

likely to recognize such experiences if they were more ready
to believe them possible?

4. Is the doctrine of the Holy Trinity an obstacle to Christian belief?

5. Wordsworth wrote in *Tintern Abbey*:

> . . . And I have felt
> A presence that disturbs me with the joy
> Of elevated thoughts; a sense sublime
> Of something far more deeply interfused,
> Whose dwelling is the light of setting suns,
> And the round ocean and the living air,
> And the blue sky, and in the mind of man;
> A motion and a spirit, that impels
> All thinking things, all objects of all thought,
> And rolls through all things.

How far is this the Christian view of God?

6. Is there any justice in the saying "The new theology
is the old heresy"?

II Revelation and the Bible

A major tragedy of evangelical life is that its forces have so often been divided in furious controversy over matters of secondary importance, of approach rather than of substance, so that believers who at heart are at one have not been able to cooperate against the common unevangelical adversary. In reaffirming the divine revelation in the Bible there is a great need for a prudent, comprehensive, and moderate approach that will not blunt its own cutting edge by too rigid or defensive an emphasis upon secondary issues.

It is a fact of experience that the conservative evangelical has more guts when it comes to Christian discipleship and personal evangelism than the so-called liberal, though he may not possess as attractive manners. The evangelical student-society on the campus, though it may often appear to outsiders somewhat self-opinionated and perhaps a little naïve in some of its affirmations, is the one among many which commonly provides lonely and puzzled students with a secure anchorage of warm Christian fellowship, and is successful in winning young men and women for Christian discipleship.

Every seminary, likewise, knows that the majority of young men and women who receive the divine call for a life of Christian service come from homes and churches that are secure in loyalty to the historic and scriptural Christian faith, and are, in this sense of the word, "conservative." So-called liberal Christianity may produce seminarians who quite genuinely enjoy talking about religion, and who feel that to take up a scholarship and spend some years in theological study will be a pleasant and improving thing. In this praiseworthy interest they are perfectly sincere, yet they are certainly not heading toward taking up any of the Lord's tough assignments. They have no sufficient dynamic to spend and be spent in the loving and self-sacrificing care of a Christian congregation, and certainly not on the mission field. A secure grasp of the historic faith is required to summon men and women to this.

It is sad that men and women with cultivated intellectual interests, open minds, and sympathetic personalities should so often prove ineffectual in winning their fellows for Christ and sustaining the church, while inherently less attractive and gifted disciples should often be powerfully used by God. This ought not to be. The fact is that very often the so-called Fundamentalist possesses the authentic wine of the gospel in his somewhat unattractive bottle, whereas the so-called liberal possesses a very attractive and winning bottle, but it contains a phoney spirit. What is needed for the revival of evangelism in the church is the authentic wine of the Spirit, but in a more attractive bottle than we sometimes find.

Revelation

The whole ground for supposing that man can know anything for certain about God is that he has been granted a divine revelation. The Bible raises the question "Canst thou by searching find out God?" (Job 11:7). The answer is plainly No. God is infinite, man is finite. God is holy, and man is defiled. We cannot reach up to Him (Isa. 55:8-9). Yet God has through his infinite grace made something of himself assuredly known. This is the principle of revelation (Gal. 1:11-12).

God's revelation is not the disclosure of a body of doctrine by the sending of a teacher or the deposition of a sacred volume. It is a divine visit, in which in his Son incarnate God breaks in upon man's experience and makes himself known not merely by teaching something, but by doing something for man's salvation. Nevertheless, this personal encounter does communicate divine knowledge. Therefore, there is a secure body of knowledge framed in an intelligible form, which is the basis for Christian faith. This may also be called the revelation, and the chief place where it is recorded is in the Bible, which is therefore normative for Christian theology. The real divergence in the theological world is not between those who look on revelation as personal and those who look upon it as "propositional," but between those who accept it as real and reliable, and those who regard it as transient and subjective.

God makes himself known to man through experience, personal, family, social, national, international. This is a salient example of the sacramental principle that God works the spiritual through the natural. Left to himself, sinful man cannot see what God is seeking to teach through experience (Jer. 7:8-14). Therefore, by the operation of the Holy Spirit, God will inspire and quicken man's natural faculties to enable him to discern the revelation (I Cor. 2:9-11, II Pet. 1:21). This divine inspiration is not to be regarded as suspending the natural human faculties of God's messenger so as to make him less truly human, but as quickening his faculties so as to make him more fully human.

Humanist critics who are chiefly interested in the development of the mind and institutions of man have tended to place all the emphasis upon the human and natural process through which ideas of God and of right have come to expression. They sap away the divine element, and tend to leave the Christian religion as a mere set of human ideas among other human ideas. This is to make everything subjective and relative, and in effect to deny revelation. By natural reaction against this, those who are chiefly interested in establishing the certainties of religion have tended to seek to explain away the human element in the process, and to teach that God's action suspends the working of the natural human faculties in the prophets. This is to put asunder what God has joined, and can represent evangelicals as disdainful of any channels of truth apart from the Bible, and of human thought in general. This can generate the false and unfortunate impression that evangelical theology is anti-intellectual.

Natural and Revealed Religion

The wisest tradition of Christian thought has ever affirmed that there is a revelation of God to be found in the "book of nature," including human nature, and that this is to be discerned by the divine gift of reason (Ps. 19: 1-6). This is the general revelation of God, for it is not confined to the Bible or to God's people. The general revelation is the basis of natural religion, that is to say, of that general acknowledgement of the existence of God and of the moral law which is the common ground of all the higher religions (Acts 14: 15-17, 17:23-28; Rom. 1:18-21). This "religion of all reasonable men" is valuable so far as it goes. Yet it is not distinctively Christian, and does not bring the message of the gospel of Christian salvation.

Some overzealous evangelicals in their desire to affirm the

supreme value of the Bible and of the Christian revelation
have virtually denied the value of natural religion. This is
surely unwise, for it leaves the Christian gospel in a state
of isolation, suspended in an intellectual vacuum. The
wisest Christian advocacy has always been careful to affirm
that the Christian faith is inherently reasonable, and, as
such, fully acceptable to the man or woman of intellectual
integrity. This is done by showing that the unique and
saving Christian revelation, the precious portrait of Christ,
is, as it were, set in the spacious frame of a general system
of rational thought covering all the interests of human life.
The Christian affirmation that there is an overarching system
of eternal rational principles enshrined in the mind of God is
a view of existence which pays much higher tribute to the
place of reason than do skeptical systems purporting to be
"scientific" which declare that man can know nothing beyond
the sphere of his immediate experience.

The particular case of this principle is provided by the
so-called proofs of the existence of God. In very brief outline
these are as follows:

1. *The Argument from Existence.*

There is in the mind of man a clear and distinct idea of
God, the perfect Being. Therefore God must exist. The mind
of man may be likened to a mirror. In the mirror there is an
image of God, so God must exist to cast the image. It is true
that man's mind is dark and corrupted by sin. His mirror is,
as it were, cracked and spotted, so that the divine image is an
imperfect one. Yet the image is there, and cannot be explained away as an illusion. This argument will be seen to be
an act of faith in the rationality of the universe, and of man
in it. It may well be admitted that in all manner of mundane
affairs men and women may be the victims of illusion and
wishful thinking. Yet the noblest thoughts that have in-

spired the minds of the greatest of men and women all down the ages cannot be dismissed as an illusion. If the latter be the case we can have no knowledge about anything!

2. *The Argument from Design.*

If one were to find a watch upon the shore of an apparently uninhabited island, it would indicate that an intelligent being had been there at some time, because an intricate mechanism could not come into existence by the casual action of the tide, etc. So we cannot imagine that the world, with all its admirable intricacy and exactitude, has come into existence without an adequate intelligent Cause.

3. *The Argument from Purpose.*

In the development of the world one event appears naturally and rationally to lead to another. Thus a world capable of supporting organic life developed, and life then appeared. A living organism developed, capable of intelligence and moral responsibility, and these qualities awoke and man became man. It would appear that the whole process was moved from the beginning by a foreseeing intelligent purpose.

4. *The Moral Argument.*

There is in the mind of man a majestic sense that he ought to do what he knows to be right. This is a mark that there is moral law reigning over the universe.

5. *The Personal Argument.*

The climax of the whole wonderful process of development in this world is the existence of a self-conscious, thinking, feeling, and morally responsible being; that is to say, a personal being, man. The first Cause of this process must be at least as noble and developed in being as is this striking effect. So the Creator must at least be everything that we mean by personal, and presumably more so than we are.

These arguments are not strictly proofs. In these mysterious matters there is always a residual objection which can be raised with at least some show of reason. Therefore the arguments for the existence of God do not suffice to compel an unbeliever to believe.

These arguments are rather to be regarded as intellectual supports to faith. It is natural in the first place for men and women to believe, but in contact with some of the difficulties to religious faith presented by experience or skeptical argument they may be assailed by doubt. In this moment the rational arguments in favor of religious belief may go far to assure the doubter that he, as a man possessed of intelligence and intellectual integrity, can rightly go on worshiping, and praying for an increase of faith and a deepening of religious experience. The arguments can powerfully support him in his sense that religious faith is a good thing, and in his desire to win through to Christian faith. So long as this limitation is kept in mind the arguments are valuable. Natural theology is therefore an important part of Christian theology, though it does not directly concern the gospel.

The Biblical Revelation

It has always been characteristic of Christian teaching that the saving revelation of God is made through Christ, and Christ alone (Acts 4:12).[1] God's work in Christ crucified and risen could never have been discerned by the reason of man (I Cor. 2:9-10). It is a special revelation. As the

---

[1] It is not necessary on this account to consign to damnation all those who have not received the Christian revelation. It is reasonable to suppose that a good God judges all men justly according to the light they have had (Amos 3:2; Luke 12:47-48). Only God knows this, and we must not presume to judge. The safe rule is that it is the business of the preacher to declare the terms of salvation—that is faith in Christ—and leave God to judge who has fulfilled them.

Bible is the only and the sufficient record of Christ, the special and saving Christian revelation is a biblical revelation.

The inspiration and divine authority of scripture consists in the message it brings, more than in the manner in which the message was recorded. By way of example, suppose a ship in distress is sending out an SOS. There may be some static in the atmosphere, and the transmission of the signal therefore may be less than perfect. However, if the transmission is sufficiently good for the message to be received the rescuers will set off, and will set off as certainly as though reception had been technically perfect. It is indeed true, on the one hand, that the medium of transmission must be good enough for the message to get through; but, on the other hand, the authority of the message lies in its content, not in the perfection of the transmission. Something of this sort may be affirmed of the transmission of God's message in scripture.

The findings of reverent and sober biblical scholarship are surely to be accepted, that what is written in scripture is recorded in terms of the human personality and experience of the respective writers, the literary methods of the times, and their conditions of natural knowledge. If this human element were found to be obscuring the transmission of God's message, then God's plan would have miscarried, and the Bible would lack the authority designed by God. Yet this is not the case. There are indeed many things in the record of scripture which are subject to human vicissitude, and which require elucidation by careful historical scholarship. Yet the record is such that the message gets through triumphantly to those who have eyes to read. The divine authority of the Bible resides in what it has to say concerning the acts of God in history. Here it contains something which manifestly sets it apart from every other book, and constitutes it the reliable and determinative authority for Christian doctrine. The modern evangelical takes up the firmest possible stand on this principle. And the stand is in fact easier to defend in a convincing manner if one is not compelled with it to defend also a multitude of minor claims for literal inerrancy.

If one can imagine a typical modern man present at God's deliverance of his people at the Red Sea (Exod. 14:13-31), one can reasonably suppose that his account would be framed in an idiom differing from that of the biblical account. It might well contain much less of the element of apparent sheer miracle, though it would still be the account of a wonderful event. This difference would be a mark of the human element in the recording of the mighty acts of God in history. Yet this does not at all involve that the biblical account is not the record of a mighty delivering act of lasting spiritual significance for the People of God, and one of the determinative points of the history of Israel.

The circumstance that is to be discerned in the Bible itself, that there is a developing understanding of God recorded in the scriptures, leading up to Christ, does involve that some lessons are more advanced than others (Heb. 1:1-2). Yet this by no means denies the wonderful unity of scripture. It is the story of a development which the viewpoint of later times shows was leading somewhere. There is a single intelligent purpose throughout. The fact that the Hebrews felt themselves to be a "chosen people" is not by itself a matter of first importance. In the ancient world all religions were tribal or national, and every people felt that their national god was their protector. The impressive thing is that the Hebrew people in fact did show a unique genius for religion, which indicates that the God of history had indeed cast them for a special role. To say this does not mean that all Hebrews were faithful or virtuous, because, unhappily, understanding of religion does not always bring virtue or faithfulness. Yet the Hebrews did possess a unique understanding, because divine knowledge was made known to them.

It is indeed true, as the Bible itself declares (Deut. 26:5), that the Hebrews started their national story as one Semitic tribe among many, with customs and religious ideas similar to those of their neighbors. The significant thing, however, is that they did not stop in this condition. There was given to them a long succession of prophetic figures, such as did not arise in other nations. These men looked upon the national or personal experience of their own times, which was often very painful and puzzling, and were able, because their faculties were quickened and stimulated by the Holy Spirit, to learn lessons about God's nature and activity in human affairs such as ordinary men could not see. So one lesson was added to another in an intelligible order, each teacher building upon what went before, and complementing it, until the scene was prepared for Christ, who summed up what was finest in all the prophets and religious institutions of Israel (Matt. 11:10-15; Luke 20:9-13, 24:27; Heb. 1:1-2).

Thus whereas the world has learned the principles of art and philosophical argument from the Greeks, and of government and administration from the Romans, we find that almost everything of real and lasting value concerning the knowledge of God and of true religion that has come to us from antiquity has come from the Hebrews, and is enshrined in their scriptures (John 4:22).

The major issue, however, regarding the biblical revelation is certainly the question of the authenticity of the portrait of Jesus Christ in the Gospels. Let no mistake be made, the Christian faith sinks or swims by this. The Christian faith is an historic faith, essentially bringing not a teaching we have to follow or a symbol we have to admire, but the gospel of a divine saving act performed upon the plane of history. The inescapable consequence of this is that if there is no secure Jesus of history there can be no secure Christ of faith either! Thus, by way of the salient example, it is possible to have a measure of natural knowledge of the fact of Christ's resurrection without receiving the divine gift of faith in Christ risen (Luke 16:30-31). Yet it cannot be too plainly stated that the reverse is not true. A faith in the risen Christ cannot be sustained apart from a reasonable conviction that Christ's resurrection was an historical fact. This is the case both in logical theory and, as we are only too sadly aware in the church, in practical experience of Christian devotion also.

It has first to be stated that the Gospels are a selection of materials gathered together in order to convince the reader of the Christian faith. This is what the New Testament itself says (John 20:30-31). The Gospels are not to be read as collections of materials for the later writing of Lives of Christ. However, this principle of evangelical selection by no means involves, as some have too lightly assumed, that the witness to the facts is therefore unreliable. Nevertheless, the one who selects from a larger mass of information interprets.

A single example will show interpretation by selection at work. In the parable of the great feast as recorded by Matthew (22:1-14) is found the saying of our Lord regarding the man who had come in without a wedding garment. This answers to the interest of the Jewish-Christian wing of the church, which wished to emphasize the undoubted truth that loyalty to certain basic moral commands of the historic

Jewish faith is required of Christians (Acts 15:28-9). Nothing is said about this in Luke's version, but instead it is emphasized that a second invitation to outsiders is given (Luke 14:16-24). This answers to the interest of the great gentile mission, and to the "freedom party" in the church. The gentiles as well as the publicans and sinners of Israel have been called. These two Christian interests are certainly not contradictory to one another, though they present an undoubted contrast within an overall unity. By criticism of this sort we can look below the surface of the narrative as we now have it, and see something of the mind of the church at work as it transmitted the tradition.

We fully appreciate the alarm of the cautious person who at this point says: If you once allow the critic to peel one skin off the onion in this way, what is there to prevent him from taking off skin after skin, until there is no onion left? That there is good reason for this alarm is seen in the circumstance that this is exactly what the radical critic has done! Basing themselves on the dogmatic theory that the first Christians received a subjective impression of "faith" into their simple, believing minds, and then gradually constructed imaginative narratives about Jesus to symbolize this, so as to make it real to their own minds and those of their hearers, the New Testament critics have stripped off layer after layer of interpretation in the Gospel-narratives, until they have arrived at the common skeptical judgment that it is rather doubtful whether we know very much at all about the Jesus of history. This result is absolutely fatal to Christian faith.

The radical critic takes his methods of investigation to an extreme precisely because, consciously or unconsciously, he welcomes this method whereby the story of Jesus may be compressed into a closed naturalistic system, and every notion of a marvelous divine work eliminated. The error of the radical is not in his technical method as such, the careful comparison of narrative with narrative in order to form judgments as to what was the interpretative mind of the church. The error is in the desire to see life as a closed naturalistic system, and in the wrongheaded notion that a book of deep religious faith like the New Testament can be read intelligibly with this naturalistic presupposition in mind. The radical critics are not more radical because they are more learned, but because they cannot take religious faith seriously. However, the man who can believe that God did in Jesus Christ perform a wonderful saving act will take a less extreme view, more moderate, more reliable, and one which does better justice to the narrative.

The biblical Christian may therefore make bold to establish his more reasonable presuppositions. A first argument in favor of a guarded and moderate approach to the use of critical techniques is that it is impossible to imagine that the magnificent portrait of Christ displayed by the Gospels should have been constructed by the first Christians out of the group mentality of the first church. One of the greatest figures of creative intellect of the period was admittedly the apostle Paul. He has written some of the world's most influential passages of inspired spiritual and theological writing. It is hard to give higher praise than this. However, in such a document as First Corinthians, for a single example, there are places where he is avowedly doing no more than expressing his own thoughtful judgment (eg. 7:1-6, 25-40). Here he gives himself away as a man of his own time, writing to his own time and subject to the limitations of his own time. Yet where the apostle knows that he has an authentic word from the Lord it comes to us down the ages still with spiritual force (eg. 11:23-26, 15:1-22). We observe in this way that Paul, though a great prophetic soul, is forever less than his Lord. Even the apostle was not great enough to have thought out "the mind of the Lord" or the Gospel-portrait of Christ from his creative imagination, as a novelist creates a character.

The same will be found true even of the Beloved Disciple. Are we then to suppose that in the simple group mind of the early disciples there were other towering figures, of creative genius more excellent than Paul and John, now entirely lost to historical memory, who performed this feat? Rather do we have a figure like that of Mark, who strikes us as a faithful man of mediocre ability, painting in gaunt but matchless words that story of Christ going to Calvary which has captivated the reverence of the world. He wrote so infinitely above his own apparent comprehension precisely because he was not creating but reporting. The eyewitnesses had seen and could never forget. Mark had heard the eyewitnesses, and he could not forget either. The only explanation of the majesty of the narrative is substantial historical reminiscence. This is a rational presupposition to bring to the technical criticism of the New Testament.

Furthermore, we have evidence of what the group mind of the primitive church in fact produced when it did construct. The church fathers of the period immediately after the New Testament produced some very worthy Christian writing which we are glad is preserved. Yet at the best it is chiefly directed to the somewhat prosaic though most necessary tasks of ecclesiastical discipline, and the ordering of the ministry and sacraments. There is less of creative and constructive prophetic insight in these writings than in the New Testament. Furthermore, in the so-called apocryphal gospels there are many sayings of Jesus, presumably chiefly copied and adapted from our canonical Gospels. But the new matter, not found in the canonical Gospels, is normally very inferior to the New Testament in good sense and spiritual understanding. We can see from what the Christians did produce when they were on their own that they did not create the Gospel-portrait of Jesus. They recorded it.

A second argument comes from the overall inward consistency of the New Testament. We have seen that there is the human element of a difference of evangelical outlook between Matthew and Luke. So likewise there are differences of emphasis between the first three Gospels and the Fourth, between John, and Paul, and Hebrews, and the Revelation, etc. Rightly understood, these natural variations are an important testimony to the reliability of the witness of the New Testament to Christ. There is no artificial uniformity between these different constituents of the New Testament. This shows these various witnesses to be indeed independent. Yet all these variations are variations upon a single theme. They bear witness to the same Christ, and to the same faith in Christ crucified and risen. This is a mark that the witness is to an authentic historical reminiscence, not to a figment of the pious imagination.

By way of comparison, suppose a court case to have arisen out of a car-wreck. One would expect a certain variation of viewpoint between the independent evidence of various witnesses, such as the driver and a traffic cop, a bystander who is young and a driver, and an elderly person who is not, etc. This variation would show that the witnesses were indeed independent, and would add to the credibility of their witness. An artificial uniformity would provide an element of suspicion that the witnesses had put their heads together beforehand. In the case of the New Testament witness to Christ there is a rich diversity, but it is a diversity in unity. However, suppose the witnesses in court were so confused about events that it was unclear whether the accident took place on the highway or between power boats on the lake, one would then be in doubt whether the accident had occurred at all. Similarly if the New Testament were in fact the free construction of the pious imagination of various groups of Christians, one would expect enormous differences in the views of Christ presented. The witness would be so diverse that one could reasonably maintain that the Christ-event had not happened!

The evangelical can with confidence take his stand that there is in the New Testament an intelligible and substantially reliable account of the life, character, and teaching of Jesus, and, in particular, a reliable witness to his death and resurrection. It is an account such as provides sufficient foundation for a historic faith. However, the evangelical is not bound to defend the difficult proposition that there is a strict literal consistency in every saying and statement in every part, and no room for a certain diversity of apprehension of Christian faith between different schools of thought. It is possible to see, at any rate, something of the mind of the church at work in selecting and transmitting the tradition.

QUESTIONS

1. How far is it true to say that Christianity is "the religion of a book"?

2. Has modern scholarship on balance reduced the value of the Bible for you, or made it a new book?

3. Is the teaching of Bible stories to children helpful in winning them to Christian faith? Do you make any difference in this respect between different parts of the Bible?

4. Do stories of bloodshed, etc., in the Old Testament

serve as an obstacle to Christian faith? Compare your ideas on this with your judgments on imaginative secular literature.

5. What do you think would have happened in the church had it given up the Old Testament?

6. Would the Gospel have survived in the church without the written New Testament?

7. What is the chief value of the Bible, for study or for reading in worship?

III The Divine Savior

The Incarnation

The evangelical must insist that a further essential of the Christian system, without which the whole falls, and upon which there can be no compromise, is that our Lord is the unique divine incarnation, in the full historic sense of the word. He is the divine Son made man, fully human, fully divine, one real Person, the permanent union of God with his handiwork, and the personal entry of God into the history of this world (John 1:14; Heb. 1:1-8).

In scriptural Christian theology the term "incarnation" cannot be used in the loose sense it bears in some other religious systems, namely, the personification of a divine attribute. Nor can it be used in the reduced sense found in some theologies claiming to be Christian, but in which the faith is hammered into the mold of a naturalistic system. Thus we cannot allow for a moment the notion that the Gospel narrative is simply the perfect symbol of various spiritual values, or that Jesus was the supreme teacher upon whom the prophetic Spirit dwelt. In Christ is to be seen God's objective saving victory, as man, and in our world, over the guilt and power of sin (Heb. 2:9-18). The man-

41

hood of Christ is to be taken with complete seriousness (Luke 2:52, 4:1-13, 22:39-46; Heb. 4:15, 5:7-8; I John 4:2-3). Otherwise, what Christ did is not as man and for man. The divinity of Christ is equally to be taken seriously, or his action is not the saving action of God (Matt. 11:25-27; Luke 20:9-13; John 1:18, 3:16; Acts 9:20; Heb. 1:1-2). Thus the evangelical upholds the catholic creeds of the ancient church as a correct and necessary interpretation of scripture.

The Virgin Birth

One issue the thoughtful modern evangelical will wish to clarify is the relation of Christ's virgin birth to the incarnation. The critics have made it almost a matter of dogma, vehemently to be insisted on, that this traditional doctrine must be denied. The influence of the anti-supernaturalistic bias is plain here. The evangelical regards it as unscientific to come to this narrative with an invincible prejudice that a miraculous birth cannot take place, so that the story of the virgin birth "must" be an importation into Christian faith from the various legends of miraculous births which occur in non-Christian mythology.

One's attitude toward the doctrine of the virgin birth mainly depends on one's view of God. If it be assumed that the development of the human race and its religious thought is essentially a determined natural process, then the conclusion is almost inevitable that the Gospel narrative is derived from pagan mythology, and is itself mythological. However, if it is believed that the process of development is initiated by and is going on under the control of an intelligent and foreseeing God, then the legends of the pagans can reasonably be regarded as part of the general revelation of God. They are shadowy and imperfect glimpses of what God was going to do, inspired by the Holy Spirit as a part of the preparation for the Gospel. In this view the Gospel-narrative is not derived from a mythological source, but the mythology and the Gospel are both derived from the same divine source.

The important principle to remember is that the incarnation is itself the essential Christian doctrine, and that the credibility of our Lord's wonderful birth hangs upon the truth of the incarnation, not the divine nature of our Lord upon the virgin birth. It is, in principle, possible to imagine that the divine Son could have united himself with human nature begotten by a human father. One can therefore, in principle, believe in the admittedly essential doctrine of the incarnation without accepting the virgin birth as the means of the union of the divine and human in Christ. Therefore it is unwise to draw attention away from the main point by too much zeal for heresy hunting on the lesser. Nevertheless, if the fact of the incarnation itself be once accepted, the virgin birth may then be regarded by the intelligent believer as alike credible, appropriate, symbolically beautiful, and a token of our Lord's real humanity.

The candid evangelical will admit that there are certain ambiguities in the Gospel-narrative. On the one hand, the two narratives which deal with the birth of Christ both clearly affirm it (Matt. 1:18-25; Luke 1:31-35). Matthew's Gospel represents the Jewish-Christian wing of the church, which would be furthest from any inclination to adopt a story from unclean pagan mythology. Also, those brought up on the Old Testament had no traditional inclination to regard sex as dirty, or celibacy as a more holy condition than marriage, for the whole tenor of Hebrew thought was the other way. The common assertion that the doctrine grew up through the influence of wishful thinking, to safeguard our Lord's sinlessness, is entirely without foundation. Furthermore, it is at least possible that the evangelists may have known our Lord's holy mother herself, for she was a member of the church in Jerusalem (Acts 1:14). Their testimony therefore may be accepted as more credible than that of modern theorists who have only deductions from the Gospel-narrative to go on.

However, some of the material incorporated into our Gospels does seem to go back to early Christian circles that either did not know of this teaching, or else, knowing it, were prepared also to speak of Joseph in a symbolical sense as the father of Jesus, presumably for the purpose of emphasizing that the Messiah was physically of the house of David. The evangelists have not been too careful in uniting the narratives, so as to reduce everything to literal consistency. Such narratives are the two genealogies of Christ (Matt. 1:1-17; Luke 3:23-38), and also Luke 2:27 and 41, which speak of the parents of Jesus, and Luke 2:48, which represents the Virgin as saying "thy father and I." It is worth noting in passing that the circumstance that the doctrine may not have been universally known from the beginning does not logically prove it to be false. In the end the attitude of various writers to this evidence depends on the presuppositions they bring to it. Those who are anxious to eliminate the supernatural wherever possible decide against the doctrine. Those who do not have an insuperable anti-supernaturalistic bias, and who can come to the narrative with an impartial judgment, are quite likely to accept the scriptural evidence for the doctrine as on balance convincing, and as quite appropriate as the mode by which the incarnation could take place.

The Doctrine of the Cross

It must candidly be admitted that the great evangelical words *atonement, sacrifice,* and *propitiation* sometimes present a very real difficulty to the modern hearer. We cannot abandon these words, but neither can we assume—as did many of the old evangelists—that this phraseology will serve as a medium for the popular communication of Christian faith to an audience which is largely ignorant of the Bible. The words themselves need to be explained.

It may be appropriate to suggest three simple definitions, in keeping with biblical thought.

1. *Atonement.*

This is "at-one-ment," or making-at-one. The verb "to atone" could in Elizabethan English be used of persons who had quarrelled, in the sense of "to reconcile" them. Thus the word atonement occurs in the familiar King James Version of Romans 5:11, but the same Greek word is translated "reconciliation" in II Corinthians 5:18-19, and the two words mean the same. It is to be noted that the New Testament speaks of the reconciliation of man to God, not of God to man. The essential idea of the Atonement is that in Christ's life of victorious obedience, culminating in the climax of his death, God has done everything that is necessary to release man from the guilt of sin, and to break its enslaving power. He has vindicated alike the majesty of the moral law, the sinfulness of sin, and the divine forgiveness. He has made it possible for man to repent and be forgiven, and so to be accepted by God.

An outline of the chief ways in which this divine victory is presented in the New Testament is as follows. Mankind is under the sway of four leading spiritual enemies. There are the demonic powers, great and small (II Cor. 4:4; Gal.

4:3; Eph. 6:12), the curse of the law of Moses placed on the disobedient (Gal. 3:10), sin (Rom. 3:9, 5:21), and death (Rom. 5:14; I Cor. 15:26). Christ suffered as man the utmost attack of all these enemies (I Cor. 2:6-8; Gal. 4:4-5; Rom. 8:3; II Cor. 5:21; Phil. 2:8). By rising from the dead Christ showed all these enemies in utter defeat. The demonic powers were dragged off like prisoners in a Roman triumph (Col. 2:15). The curse of the law was shown to be at an end for believers (Rom. 10:4). The spell of temptation to sin was broken (Rom. 6:10, 8:3; I Cor. 15:56-57). Death, the last enemy of mankind, was conquered (Rom. 6:9-10; I Cor. 15:55-57).

2. *Sacrifice.*

Sacrifice in the Old Testament is the offering to God of an object set apart by sacred custom as an "acted prayer" that the worshiper is offering himself, and all that he has, in consecration to God. It is also sharing a sacred meal with God, as a means of fellowship with him. Thus, in the general sense, a sacrifice is the means provided by God whereby man may offer himself to God, and have communion with God. Christ's life and death of sinless obedience, offered to the Heavenly Father by the divine Son-made-man, is the supreme, final, and spiritually efficacious means of doing this. Therefore the cross is the supreme sacrifice. This is particularly worked out in the Epistle to the Hebrews. The divine Son (1:2-3) made himself fully one with us (2:14, 17). As one of us he conquered in a sinless life (4:15), offering the sacrifice of obedience (5:5-8). This is the sacrifice of the New Covenant of inward spiritual religion (8:6-12). The ascended Christ, still human, and man's representative before God, is the heavenly High Priest who offers this sacrifice (4:14, 7:23-27, 8:1-2; 9:11-12, 15,

12:24), which opens the door for true spiritual access to God (9:24-26, 10:19-22).

3. *Propitiation.*

Propitiation, also translated *expiation*, is the means provided by God whereby that which is offensive to his holy nature is cleansed. In early Bible times it largely had a ritual connotation, as of the wiping away of ceremonial uncleanness (eg. Num. 8:21 NEB). As it was increasingly realized that what is offensive to God is not ritual taboo but moral guilt, the word took on a higher meaning, and in the New Testament bears the deeper spiritual and ethical sense of "the means by which the barrier of guilt between man and God is broken down" (Rom 3:25; compare KJV and NEB; I John 2:2, 4:10).

The Resurrection

The head-on collision between the essentially unbelieving attitude to Christianity, which sees salvation as not more than a matter of psychological suggestion, adjustment, and release, and the essentially God-centered attitude, which affirms salvation to be the result of a historic saving work of divine grace, comes to its clearest demonstration at this point. It is for this reason that the New Testament assumes throughout that belief in Christ's resurrection is the chief test for Christian faith (I Cor. 15:12-19).

The essential incarnational principle of historic and scriptural Christianity is that God works the spiritual through the natural. The focus of this principle is that his divine Son became truly man in this world, and lived a real sacrificial life of victorious obedience, even to the cross. The climax of this life and death is the glorious resurrection, which is God's triumphant act of "more-than-reversal" of Christ's death (Rom. 6:8-9). This is the divine token that the death upon the cross is in fact God's mysterious victory of power and love (Acts 2:22-36), and is not, as the world naturally sees it to be, God's decisive defeat. The evangelical affirms that if there was no resurrection, there is no victory, and therefore no gospel of grace.

The reason the unbelieving world is determined to deny the resurrection if it can is plain. If this marvelous divine act can be allowed, it is impossible to defend the view that the world in which we live is a closed system. It is then impossible to keep God out. The critical reconstructor of Christian theology cannot accept the New Testament witness to the empty tomb because it is a physical miracle, and a marvelous divine action within the sphere open to examination by the physical sciences is to be regarded as quite impossible in principle. So the critic will conduct a convenient strategic withdrawal into the immaterial sphere of the human mind, where physicists with measures and cameras cannot follow. It can be allowed by the critic that God did in Christ perform a work, but *only in the mind*. The disciples became aware—immediately, powerfully, and mysteriously—that the invisible Jesus was triumphant over death, and their pious imagination constructed the Gospel narrative in order vividly to symbolize their faith, focus it for themselves, and communicate it to others. Yet in point of fact the body of Jesus lay moldering in the grave. The incarnation is true for faith but false in fact, a denial of both the rational and incarnational principles.

This familiar modern compromise is an unstable one in two ways. On the one hand, the consistent and clear-sighted unbeliever will certainly include the immaterial sphere of the human mind as part of his naturalistic system. The same form of so-called scientific argument that will affirm that it is impossible for a physical body to disappear into another form will also be found affirming that the mind of man is a complicated chemical and electrical reaction set up by the development of the physical organism. The strategic withdrawal of faith from the physical to the mental is not in fact possible. The withdrawal gives too much away.

On the other hand, the consistent and clear-sighted believer will have no difficulty in accepting the possibility of a marvelous divine act within the physical world, full of spiritual significance—a miracle in fact. All the feats of applied science are examples of events happening in the physical world, full of meaning, which would not have happened had nature been left to herself. The human thinking mind has not indeed broken or suspended the laws of nature, but by understanding them has worked through them. If our minds can do this to a small extent, then the infinite mind of God can do it even to the wonder of the empty tomb. The evangelical, therefore, can do what the naturalistic critic cannot do. He can come to the scriptures without an overwhelming bias in his interpretative theories against the supernatural, and so can allow the New Testament to speak for itself.

The wise evangelical will candidly allow that the accounts of the resurrection bear upon them the mark of writers who were trying to witness to an event so unparalleled and wonderful that they had no words adequate to describe it. This circumstance does not call the narrative into question, for if a rising from the dead had actually taken place this is just what one would expect in the account of it. So we are not surprised that the story is pervaded by an atmosphere of wonder, rather than of pedestrian common sense. Our faith need not therefore be offended by the variations in the Gospel accounts. Matthew and John record resurrection-appearances both in Jerusalem and Galilee (Matt. 28:9-10,

16-20; John 20:11-29, 21:1-14), Mark (apparently) in Galilee only (Mark 16:6-8), and Luke in Jerusalem only (Luke 24:13-53), while Matthew and Mark speak of one angel at the tomb (Matt. 28:1-6; Mark 16:5), and Luke and John of two (Luke 24:4; John 20:11-13). Clearly, behind our present Gospels there were independent narratives, not exactly alike in detail, and the evangelists have not been careful to tidy up every detail, as though they were modern research-workers. Broadly speaking, the variety in detail and independence of the original narratives speak of the agreement and conviction of the primitive church in witness to the essential great fact, and to the validity of the four Gospels rather than the reverse.

Finally, the cautious evangelical, who is prepared to let scripture speak for itself, will not pontificate beyond scripture regarding the precise nature of Christ's resurrection-body.

The essential which the scriptural theologian will insist upon is that evangelical faith does not, when properly understood, speak of the resuscitation of a corpse! We wipe off this common critic's slur. At the same time, to affirm this by no means involves, as is so often assumed, that the tomb was not empty. Christian faith must see the resurrection as a triumphant "more-than-reversal" of death, which took place within our world. Yet this involves much more than the bare return to life of the body which had died on the cross. The resurrection was not the mere reassembling of a physical frame of carbon, hydrogen, oxygen, calcium, etc. Nor was the risen Christ an invalid recovering from a shattering physical ordeal. The tomb was empty, yet the body had not been taken away (Matt. 27:62-66; Mark 16:6; Luke 24:12, 22-24; John 20:1-10). The shameful death was reversed. The death was more than reversed, for the body had taken on a new form answering alike to the humility of the body which had died and also to the glory of the realm of God (Luke 24:15-16; John 20:24-28). He was the same Person, yet at times they could hardly recognize him, and he could appear and disappear (Luke 24:30-31; John 20:19-26). This reconstruction of events is admittedly mysterious, but it is what one finds if one takes the narratives seriously.

Paul, speaking in I Corinthians 15 of the general resurrection of believers in terms of the one resurrection which had actually taken place, is forced into the paradox of a "spiritual body," which authentically corresponds to the body that has died, yet which is a body such as *can* "inherit the kingdom of God" (vv. 42-54). And the rational Easter-faith of those who follow the New Testament is surely that Christ's resurrection-body was "a glorious body." It fully corresponded to the body that had died, even to "the mark of the nails," yet is possessed the glory of the spiritual sphere. This is not the survival of a spirit, with the body moldering in the grave, but a triumph over death accomplished by God within the order of this world. This is a mysterious subject. Yet the mystery is in keeping with what one would rationally expect of God's mightiest act in working the spiritual through the natural.

The Ascension

The main point which the thoughtful modern evangelical will emphasize here is that belief in Christ's ascension does not involve the notion that heaven is a place, or that it is "up."

That which is beyond time and space and common-sense experience cannot be described in matter-of-fact language. Symbolical language has to be employed. The symbolism appropriate to the notions of divine majesty and sovereignty over the universe is that of exaltation, i.e., the sense of "up," as in "lift up your hearts." Simple and unreflective believers, either in biblical times or in the present day, with minds unaccustomed to abstractions, may sometimes have imagined the seat of God's majesty as some kind of place above the sky. Nor is there any spiritual harm in this, within the circle of the unreflective. However, it is most unfair to the mature theologians of the church, either in the more distant or the more recent past, to affirm that they have taught that the risen and ascended Christ possessed some sort of *material* body such as could occupy space, or that heaven is a place, when they have employed the inevitable language of exaltation.

It is all too easy and too common for modern critics, particularly those with that "little knowledge" which is a dangerous thing, to speak superciliously of the "three-story universe" imagined by the biblical and early Christian writers, and to dismiss what these writers have to say as having no contact with our superior mentality. The Bible writers were just as aware as we are that God does not have a material body, and that the seat of his majesty is not in any kind of place (I Kings 8:27; Psalm 139:7-10), though they may have expressed themselves in a way different from ours.

It is not necessary to dismiss the story of Christ's ascension in Acts 1:4-11 as nothing more than the construction of the imagination of the early church, though it does not follow that an observer with the typical modern mentality, if such an one can be imagined as present, would have described this mysterious event in just the same language as we have in the Bible. Our Lord appeared from time to time in his glorious resurrection-body, and disappeared, until the church had thoroughly learned that he was present all the time, whether they could see him or no (John 20:19-29, 21:4-7;

Acts 1:1-3; I Cor. 15:3-7). This stage of Christ's historic work must needs come to an end, however, for the Lord of the church is to be thought of as a universal Person, and not as a particular human shape associated with first-century Palestine. Nothing is more spiritually appropriate than that his last momentous disappearance should be not just that he *vanished*, but that he vanished in this particular manner, and in such a way as to symbolize that the reason he is to be seen no more by the church in his glorified humanity is that he is seated upon the throne of the Majesty of the universe (Eph. 1:20-23, 4:8-10; Heb. 9:24-28).

QUESTIONS

1. Would the Gospel record be easier to believe if it contained fewer miracle-stories? If it were easier to believe would it produce more Christian faith?

2. Has the activity of New Testament scholarship in seeking to recover a reliable historical picture of the life and times of Jesus assisted Christian faith, or made it harder?

3. Does the virgin birth appear to you to guarantee our Lord's human nature, or to call it in question?

4. Does what is outlined in this book regarding the death of Christ still allow us to sing:

> But we believe it was *for us*
> He hung and suffered there.[1]

5. What appeals to you most as a guarantee of Christ's resurrection: (a) the evident reliability of the Gospel-narra-

[1] Cecil F. Alexander, "There Is a Green Hill Far Away."

tive? (b) that the enemies of the infant faith did not produce the body of Jesus? (c) the courage and dynamic witness of the church? (d) the endurance of the church since, and the good which the Christian faith has produced?

6. Is it right to sing of Jesus

> I wish that His hands had been placed on my head,
>   That His arms had been thrown around me,
> And that I might have seen His kind look when He said,
>   "Let the little ones come unto me."? [*]

7. How can we translate "bondage to demonic powers" into intelligible modern terms?

---

[*] Jemima T. Luke, "I Think When I Read That Sweet Story."

IV Life in the Spirit

The Holy Spirit

The chief truth which the evangelical would emphasize is that "Holy Spirit" is not, as in much Christian humanist literature, a metaphor for the higher faculties of human nature. A cardinal doctrine of the Christian faith is that when God by his grace makes a man or woman different in character and conduct he does so by the indwelling of a personal influence. It is a process analogous to the manner in which a human friend of noble moral character can lift those around him to a higher level simply by being with them in loving, sympathetic, and self-sacrificing companionship. The personal indwelling by the Spirit is, however, far more intimate and far more prevailing. Thus the private life and devotion of the believer is "the walk of the soul with God," and when Christians meet for worship they are not just a company coming to meet other men and women, and to listen to someone talk. It is a common but profound error to think of public worship as though it were a sort of dignified public meeting. There is always an unseen *Person* there, and he constitutes the gathering.

The term "Holy Spirit" is a striking Old Testament

metaphor to convey the idea of God in action in the world. It is a comparison drawn from human experience. While a man lives he breathes, and when he exerts himself he breathes strongly. Therefore the "breath" is the "life." The Living God therefore has a "Strong Breath," or Spirit, breath and spirit being the same word. So it is natural to find that God's most special manifestations of himself, and his most prevailing actions, are described as the work of the "Spirit of the Lord." Such are the act of creation itself (Gen. 1:2; Ps. 33:6; Isa. 40:13), the calling and equipment of prophets and heroes (Judg. 6:34, 14:6; Isa. 61:1; Ezek. 11:5), and the divine equipment of the Messiah (Isa. 11:2). The coming of the messianic Kingdom was expected to be accompanied by a great outpouring of the prophetic Spirit (Joel 2:28-29). Considered as a man, our Lord himself is the climax of the prophets. Therefore the Spirit came upon Jesus to equip him for his public and prophetic ministry (Mark 1:9-12; Heb. 1:8-9).

In light of this, the Holy Spirit in the New Testament is the personal agent whereby God as he is known in Jesus Christ makes his presence known, fulfilling thereby Christ's promise, "Lo, I am with you alway" (Matt. 28:20). Christ is the Paraclete or *Advocate* (I John 2:1), that is, the influential friend who comes along to "show one the ropes." Another rendering of the same word is *Comforter*, that is, "the one who makes one strong" (Latin *fortis* = strong). So the Holy Spirit is a divine Presence with the church, like Christ, only belonging to every time and place, and there is no one to see (John 14:16). Thus the Spirit of God is also the Spirit of Christ (Rom. 8:9). One cannot in experience distinguish between the Holy Spirit and the indwelling Christ, though there is a distinction in thought. The divine Spirit is the one who *now applies* in living personal conviction the effect of what the divine Son *did once for all,* and for the world (I Cor. 12:3). His divine operation is the connecting link between historic faith and present experience.

Conversion

In turning to consider the more immediate work of the Spirit in the heart of the believer we must first consider *conversion.* This is a word covering all the various aspects of that personal decision "to turn . . . from the power of Satan unto God" (Acts 26:18) which marks the beginning of the life of mature evangelical faith. However, the necessity of conversion by no means involves that Christian nurture from childhood is not a very important influence, which ought to lead to mature Christian faith (II Tim. 1:5).

Repentance

The well-tried evangelical pattern for entrance upon the mature Christian life of full decision for Christ is that it begins with a conviction of sin, leading to repentance (Luke 7:44-48, 15:7, 18-24, 18:13-14; Acts 8:22, 11:18; Rom. 3:19-20, 7:9-13; II Cor. 7:10). Repentance is not the regret that one is not a better man—which can be experienced by any candid soul—or even the remorse that Judas felt (Matt. 27:3-5). Repentance involves a completely sincere purpose actually to turn away from evil to good (Isa. 1:16-20, Luke 19:8-9).

One of the greatest barriers to the preaching of the gospel today is that the modern man is not worrying about his sins. He is certainly worrying, perhaps more than ever before, about those disorders of society which may make the world an unpleasant place in which to live. So he is running off by the millions to psychologists to seek release, or to drugs to find a temporary and spurious escape. The secular-minded man certainly does not arrive at any sort of peace of mind, yet he is not deeply concerned about his standing as a guilty man before the holy God. This unreality of outlook stands perhaps as the chief obstacle to the spread of the gospel and the healing of mankind.

A leading problem of the modern evangelical is how he may bring his hearers to a rightful sense of personal guilt before the God of holy love. He cannot do it by hell-fire preaching! Nor was this ever the best way. Though our Lord believed in hell (Matt. 10:28), he was certainly not a "hell-fire preacher." The awful consequences of final impenitence were in his teaching a grim foreboding in the background, not held out as a major reason for doing good. The greatest evangelists have followed this emphasis, and we should do so today.

So we hear sermons furiously denouncing the social sins of the people who most probably are not in church, and the congregation goes home glowing with self-righteousness: Thank God *I* am not a racist, and I *have* voted for reforming measures! This too often passes for the social witness of the church, making it harder for the congregation to repent. The wise evangelical will speak rather of the greatness of the love of God toward us, of the joy and excellence of the life of loving fellowship with God, of the searching character of God's call, of the absolute obligation we have in return to give ourselves wholly to his love and obedience, and of the dreadful fact that we have not done so.

The Need of Salvation

The chief interest of the evangelical in this matter today is to establish and make intelligible to the modern hearer that the discoveries of organic evolution and the modern exposi-

tion of the Genesis Fall-story have in no way discredited what
the Bible has to say about sin, and have not in the slightest
explained away man's need of a Savior.

It is important to remember that the Bible is a
book of practical devotion and obedience, rather than of
philosophical speculation. The Bible does not attempt to
explain in theory *why* sin should exist in a world made and
ruled by a good God. Rather is it concerned to open men's
eyes to the way in which sin actually works, how dishonor-
able it is to God, and how degrading to man. Thus in
Genesis there is no explanation of why there should have
been a Tempter, and why Adam and Eve should so unac-
countably and inexcusably have listened to his plea. Instead,
the condition of the human heart is traced out with masterly
spiritual and psychological insight. The originating principle
of sin is seen in pride, the desire of man to use his powers
to lift himself above his rightful condition of reverence for
God and dependence upon God, and to live his own life in
his own way (Gen. 3:1-6). Having done this, man discovers
instead that he is naked and ashamed, separated from God by
a guilty conscience (Gen. 3:7-11). The next stage is that
men and women blame one another (Gen. 3:11-13). By the
natural chain of cause and effect this leads in the next gen-
eration to murder, and then to vainglorious cities, to corruption, and to war (Gen. 4:3-13, 19-24, 6:1-7, 11:1-9).

This is an illuminating picture of the human condition,
though those who are wise in their own eyes will wriggle
every way rather than admit it. Thus in our own time mankind awoke to a wonderful new power, atomic energy. In
principle it could be used for good or evil. However, by a
certain grim inevitability in a world given to self-assertion
rather than to reverence for God the natural first use of this
power was for the possessor vaingloriously to exalt himself

over his enemy. This left all the world chilled with fear, and men began to wish the power had never been discovered. Likewise, effective contraception, which might be used to exalt the dignity of family life, has in fact largely been used by pleasure-seekers to make the world safe for fornication, and to repudiate God's marriage law. Endless other examples suggest themselves to us. The process of the Fall goes on all the time.

When Paul writes, "For as in Adam all die, even so in Christ shall all be made alive" (I Cor. 15:22), he does not mean that a contamination has been carried to all the race by natural procreation. If this were the sense of the scripture it might have been shaken by biological discovery. What Paul intends is far more profound and spiritual than this. Adam (the name means 'the man,' which is the reason Paul mentions him in this passage) is the representative man, whose action portrays what the race has done as a whole, and every individual man and woman within the race. Man in his pride has lifted himself up against God, has disobeyed, and therefore "died," i.e. has ruined himself and his world. Thus Paul does not say that all men die because they have inherited a depraved condition from their first parents, but because they have all sinned (Rom. 5:12). But they have all sinned because they are part of a race that collectively is spiritually represented by Adam.

Faith

In the past the evangelical has chiefly felt himself called upon to emphasize that full Christian saving faith is much more than acceptance of a body of doctrine, no matter how correct. It is the faith that works by love, (Gal. 5:6), issuing in trust and obedience. However, the real battle today is on the opposite front. This is the occasion of some real evangelical confusion.

The tendency of the so-called reconstructors of theology is to argue that there is no actually existing sovereign God, no actual historic saving work performed by God on the plane of history in his Son-made-man, crucified and risen. There is in fact no revealed authoritative body of truth, no scriptural orthodoxy. There are only the ever-changing subjective impressions and mental symbols of the first Christians, then of the writers of the New Testament, and of Christians since. The business of the evangelical (and of the Catholic) is to affirm that, while Christian faith is certainly not the same thing as acceptance of a body of doctrine, it can not possibly be held without the acceptance in one's mind of certain essential Christian truths.

A classic definition of evangelical saving faith was given by Wesley: "It is not barely a speculative, rational thing, a cold, lifeless assent, a train of ideas in the head; but also a disposition of the heart." [1] The error of institutional and formal religion has ever been to say in effect: Faith is not a mere subjective disposition of the heart. It is authoritative orthodoxy. It is a train of ideas in the head.

The error of the modern reconstructors of theology is in the opposite direction. In their fear of attaching the label of Christian faith to anything that could be proved or disproved scientifically, in effect they say: Faith is not a system of ideas in the head. It is an existential experience. It is a disposition of the heart.

The difficulty is that if the intelligent man once becomes convinced that there is not anything really there the disposition of the heart will fade away. The true evangelical will

[1] John Wesley, Sermon I, "Salvation by Faith."

keep the two sides firmly together, the secure historic revelation and the movement of the heart toward it. The rule is "not only, but also." Evangelical saving faith is the movement of the affections, the emotions, and the moral will toward the reasonably believed facts of the historic creed (Heb. 11:6).

Justification

This great evangelical word means "acquittal in God's court." It represents the free forgiveness of the penitent sinner, but expressed in legal language (Luke 18:9-14; Rom. 1:17; Gal. 2:16).

The notion that justification is a bare change of status before God, a sort of formal transaction, a legal fiction, even a solemn pretense is a leading misunderstanding. This is certainly not the doctrine of scripture. "Justification by faith and not by the works of the law" does not involve that God, having forgiven the sinner, is then content to leave him as he is. This scriptural formula simply means that Christianity is not a revived and purified Phariseeism, which leaves man to save himself by self-imposed obedience to the law of God.

The chief fetter that prevents men and women from rising above their dead selves to better things is the sense of moral unworthiness, the load of a guilty conscience, the despairing feeling: My hands are not clean enough to meddle in holy things, and give myself to the service of God. Therefore, to know that one is freely forgiven by God, *accepted* by God when one can do nothing to merit acceptance, ought to work in the soul a great new spring of moral energy and courage. Thus justification ought to bring the first decisive step toward a cleansing of inward character, a release from moral frustration, and a life renewed in constructive moral conduct. If this profound moral change, inward and outward, worked by the Holy Spirit, does not begin, then faith is not evangelical saving faith, and the man is not truly justified. There is no principle upon which the wise evangelical will insist more strongly than this. Christianity is essentially a moral religion (Rom. 3:31, 6:1-7, 15-22; Gal. 5:16-25).

Assurance

It is the privilege of the Christian, and an essential part of the spiritual equipment of every effective Christian worker, that he be assured of the presence, power, and goodness of God, and that he is on the path to final salvation if he holds firmly to the Lord in the devotional and moral discipline of the Christian life. The evangelical must revive the witness within the church to this truth.

A leading and clear exposition of the doctrine of assurance is however based on Romans 8:16: "The Spirit itself beareth witness with our spirit, that we are the children of God." This text speaks of two witnesses. There is the witness of my own spirit, which is the commonsense moral argument: Since I closed with Christ in faith I am so deeply aware of a transformation of my inward character and outward conduct that I cannot bring myself to doubt that the Holy Spirit is at work in my heart. This experience is indispensable to every sincere believer. To claim any form of full assurance without the moral change is a dangerous delusion. There is also the witness of the Holy Spirit, which is an immediate and mysterious impression on the soul. It belongs to the sphere of the heart and affections, as the other witness does to the moral will. When this witness of inward security, peace, and normally of humble penitent joy is joined to the awareness of moral change, so that the two chime together, then and only then is the believer lifted to the full privilege of the Christian, namely, to full assurance. However, this assurance brings with it no guarantee that the Christian will not fall into spiritual loss, if he does not carefully walk with Christ in devotional and moral discipline. Thus as Wesley said, "he is saved from the fear though not from the possibility of falling away from the grace of God." [2]

QUESTIONS

1. Why do people so often speak of the Holy Spirit as "It"? Is there any harm in this?

2. The friends of Cornelius had been converted. Why did they then need to be baptized (Acts 10:44-47)? Is someone who has been baptized but not converted a Christian? Were such as the young Luther and Wesley Christians before their evangelical experiences?

3. Is it better to have been brought up as a Christian in a "good" home, or to be brought up a pagan in a tough home, and then wonderfully converted? What is the background, in this respect, of great Christian leaders of the present of whom you can think?

4. "Thou hast conquered, O pale Galilean; the world has grown grey from Thy breath." [3] Do you think that this is a fair judgment on the world before and after Christ?

5. Why do so many worried people go to a psychiatrist in preference to a pastor?

6. Do you think that the idea of evolution has taken away from our reverence for the Genesis Fall-story? or that it has decreased our sense of sin?

[2] *Ibid.*
[3] Swinburne, *Hymn to Proserpine.*

7. Is religious faith easier for people who are not too bright?

8. Do you think that evangelists, by and large, have gone astray in stressing stern morality too little? or too much?

9. Do you know many people who have an assurance of their salvation? What is your candid opinion of them as Christians?

V Christianity in Earnest

An air of joyous victory breathes through New Testament Christianity. The first Christians possessed nothing in numbers, prestige, money, influence, or security (II Cor. 6:1-10), yet they were conquerors of the world. How sadly different are some of our churches today, with all their numbers, wealth, and learning, and with preachers—not to say people —painfully uncertain as to what to believe, what is the purpose of life, and how they are to receive strength to fight in its battle. The witness of the evangelical is that this secret of victory is not something that is organized by commissions, taught in seminaries, or promoted by publicity. It is the gift of God, granted to the faithful.

The New Testament Christians form a close, disciplined, cohesive, and sustaining fellowship because in Christ they have come to a decisive change in life (I John 3:14). The life of a Christian is marked with serene confidence (Acts 4:13). Christians are not afraid to be swimmers against the tide of society (Acts 5:26-29; I Cor. 4:10-14), and they count it a privilege to suffer persecution for the name of Christ (Acts 5:41-42; II Cor. 4:7-18). This martyrdom is not the tragic miscarriage of God's plan. It is his plan, whereby the believer is to be made fully one with his suffering Lord, in His cross and His victory (Mark 8:31-37; I Peter 3:13-18, 4:12-16). The individual believer likewise enjoys a splendid sense of conquest over his own lower nature, and a great liberty to serve God (Rom. 8:1-6; I Cor. 6:9-11).

As the church expanded, however, and became with the passage of time a communal religion embracing a large proportion of nominal members, this victory and this spirit of discipline were largely lost. This is the condition of the church as we too often see it today. One of the chief duties of the consistent evangelical is to keep alive in the church the witness to original New Testament Christianity, and to rebuke the common notion that the most which can be expected of the Christian is a measure of conventional morality a little higher than that which passes in the general body of society. We do not disown the easygoing multitude, but we stand for "Christianity in earnest."

Regeneration

Regeneration, or the "new birth," is a scriptural term for the first decisive stage of the life of evangelical faith (John 3:1-7). We have seen above that *justification*—that is, forgiveness—is this step considered from the point of view of man's first acceptance by God, and spiritual standing with God. The *new birth* is this same step considered from the point of view of the actual moral change which then starts. Thus regeneration is the first step in the process of sanctification.

Sanctification; Holiness

These words have been loved in evangelical tradition, yet they have also come to have unhelpful associations in the minds of many of our people. Therefore it is most necessary for evangelicals to preach the doctrine with renewed conviction, though it may be wise in popular communication to avoid these words, and to render the sense of the New Testament into other terms.

In the first place, there is frequent confusion between "sanctification" and "entire sanctification." Sanctification is the New Testament term for that progressive moral change of inward character and outward conduct worked by the Holy Spirit, starting at justification or forgiveness, which is the essential mark of the life of every sincere believer (Rom. 6:6-17; Gal. 5:22-26; Titus 3:7-8; James 2:14-17). The evangelical cannot allow anyone to call in question the need for sanctification, or the essential connection between justification and sanctification. The Christian faith is an ethical religion, or it is nothing (Matt. 5:17-19, 7:21-27, 25: 31-46).

Holiness is the name given to the due and expected climax of the gradual growing process of sanctification (Matt. 5:43-48, 19:16-21). Hence it can also be called entire sanctification. The evangelical of today needs to exercise discretion as well as determination in this matter, for these kindred terms have been the subject of frequent misunderstanding, unhappy and needless controversy, and consequent mutual impoverishment among evangelicals. The mainspring of misunderstanding is the preaching of holiness as though it were essentially an emotional climax rather than a moral experience. This is quite false to scripture and to the wisest teaching in the church about holiness. It has indeed been held by many that the divine gift of holiness may be expected to come in a sudden dramatic flash of insight, as it were, parallel to conversion. For this reason it has been often called the "second blessing." Nothing in the idea of a sudden experience of enlightenment and victory is in itself objectionable or improbable, for all processes of illumination and decision commonly work up to a climax. However, if the emphasis upon holiness as "sudden" be linked with an emphasis upon holiness as chiefly emotional, the impression can then too easily be created that this form of preaching is akin to mass hysteria. In consequence, conventionally minded churchmen, desiring social and intellectual respectability, have commonly fought shy of this important part of the gospel.

The Christian cannot indeed expect in this life to be lifted clean above every human limitation, so as to be freed entirely from temptation, or from spiritual and moral mistakes due to genuine ignorance, inexperience, or surprise. This sort of sinless perfection is reserved for heaven, and to claim it in this life reflects a dangerous lack of self-knowledge (Phil. 3:12). What the earnest Christian can expect is that the grace of God will so strengthen him that he will not dally with sin in his secret heart, and defile himself, and then have to go back to God in shame. If temptation presents itself his heart will turn away in spontaneous loathing. If he is entrapped by inexperience into an error he will not cling to it in pride, but will learn that lesson, repent, and sin that way no more. Therefore his heart will be at rest within, in secure spiritual victory. Thus the climax of growth in grace is "*entire* victory over all *willful* sin." It was in line with this that Wesley wisely disowned the proposition of sinless perfection, and defined Christian perfection, or holiness, as "perfect love."

An important proviso regarding the preaching of holiness is that reticence and modesty regarding one's own spiritual endowments, and a painful awareness of how easy it is for the human heart to deceive itself (Jer. 17:9), are sure marks of the truly good man or woman. It therefore seems inherently likely that the saints who come nearest to the divine gift of perfect love will be very cautious in claiming it for themselves. If they do, it will only be in fear and trembling, lest they deny the gift of God, and certainly not "unadvisedly, lightly, or wantonly."

Yet the gift of perfect love must be believed in and expected, for the alternative is the sad conclusion that compromise with willful sin is, in principle, inevitable in the Christian life, no matter how sincerely one is committed in faith to Christ. This is to put a limit to the saving grace of God, and to say that God cannot "save to the uttermost" (Heb. 7:25). This admission, if made, blunts the cutting edge of Christian morality, fatally reducing it from the heroic and world-defying to the conventional.

Moral Law or Social Creed

It is at this point that Christian morality, personal and social, joins Christian faith. This union provides one of the chief issues to which the thoughtful evangelical must devote careful thought, and make a bold witness.

One of the saddest and most frustrating elements in the present religious situation is the widespread assumption that a Christian who is loyal to the principles of the historic scriptural Christian faith (and is, in this good sense of the word, "conservative") is likely also to be a conservative in the sense of being timid and reactionary in the social witness of the Christian church. And our unevangelical opponents in the church therefore try to press the converse proposition: namely, that to be an effective and progressive Christian citizen one will naturally take the emphasis off the preaching of the historic faith of salvation by divine grace. This is another damaging example of putting asunder what God has joined, to mutual impoverishment. The modern evangelical will advance the proposition that it is perfectly possible to be orthodox in theology and also progressive in social thought.

We face the tragic paradox of our times. Never was there a day when there was more widespread awareness of the need for social reform and improvement: international peace, assistance for undeveloped nations, control of population explosion, preservation of the environment, slum clearance, education, etc. The Christian will welcome all these, and similar movements, as good and hopeful, and as the marks of the work of the Holy Spirit in human society. The Christian citizen will certainly join with his fellow citizens of good will to help in all these righteous causes. Yet together with this heightened social awareness there is in all the "free," "progressive," and affluent nations a constant decline of public morality. And it would often seem that the more favored the society, the swifter the decline.

Thus together with more social resolve we have more dishonesty, more crimes of violence, more fornication, more VD, more broken homes and divorce, more smut in popular amusements and novels, more commercially organized pornography, more alcoholism and drug addiction, more irrational rebellion against the decencies of home and community life—all influences which, if they go far enough, cause the corruption and eventual dissolution of civilization. This tragic and irrational paradox demonstrates the total bankruptcy of social resolve. Man is not able to regenerate himself or his society out of his own resources, by better material conditions of life and more education.

The grim scriptural judgment upon the community of the men of this world as they seek to live their self-contained lives upon some basis other than reverence for the Sovereign God is that they will inevitably bring upon themselves fiery indignation and overflowing ruin (Mic. 3:9-12; Luke 19:41-44; Rev. 18). This view is not a figment of the imagination of backward-looking and defensive "horse-and-buggy" revival preachers, hopelessly out of communication with the modern man and the modern world. It is a realistic view of the world situation as it develops practically before our eyes, though those who discard the viewpoint of Scripture rarely have vision enough to understand their own times.

QUESTIONS

1. Do you think that you would find it easier to maintain Christian standards as a member of a small, strict, and unpopular group running the risk of persecution, or as a member of a large, easygoing church in a nominally Christian society?

2. Do you find in your experience that professing Christians possess more resources of cheerful courage in face of trouble than do the generality of people? Why does the world seem to look upon ministers of religion as solemn killjoys?

3. It would seem that at the present time, and on a world view, the biggest advances of popular evangelism are being made by "holiness-type" churches. Can you suggest a reason? Does popular success prove that they are right?

4. Have you ever met anyone who claimed to have received the gift of holiness, or entire sanctification? Did you take his testimony seriously?

5. Have attempts to improve public morality by legislation on balance done more harm than good? Think of examples in different spheres of life.

6. Would a prohibition law (of alcohol) become socially right if there were enough public opinion behind it to enforce it in a satisfactory manner? Would a law permitting

bigamy become socially right if there were enough public opinion to demand it?

7. Should one choose a candidate to vote for principally on account of his piety and high standard of private morality, or on account of his program?

8. Is it right for a Christian citizen to take time off from church meetings to go to political meetings or committees, labor union meetings, etc.?

9. "One nation under God"—if this principle is abandoned, what other basis can you suggest for the state?

VI The Church and Sacraments

Protagonists of the church who speak of "organized Christianity" often lay too much emphasis upon the *organization*; that is to say, upon the familiar ecclesiastical structure, with its officers with their positions to maintain, with its property and rights to defend, with its budget to balance. This emphasis is an unevangelical one, and evangelists who behave as though their chief motive was to increase their congregation, and by consequence the prestige and income of their group, have sadly strayed from the truth.

It may well be that for a long time to come, while Christian faith is fighting to maintain its witness in a secularized society, the organization of religion will center less around large public congregations, spacious church buildings, and paid professional clergy, than it has sometimes done in the past. To the evangelical this is not necessarily the decline of the church. These external things may be very good and helpful in their time and in their proper place, and the evangelical is not against maintaining them. Yet they are not essentials to the church. In their greatest and most triumphant days the evangelical denominations were largely without these things. What the evangelical regards as of permanent and vital importance is the underlying principle of the *disciplined* church, and the *visible* church. Spiritual discipline is the living organism. Organization is only the skeleton. And it is the discipline which matters, not the organization.

If it once be granted that the essence of the Christian life is to confess faith in Christ, to witness to this faith before the world, to live in conscious personal fellowship with him, and to exercise a life of responsible personal love toward others in the fellowship, it then follows that Christians must systematically meet together and tenaciously stick together, and must come together for the sake of definite acts of worship and of prayer (Matt. 5:14-16; Acts 4:5-21; Heb. 10:23-25). To the Christian these sacred moments of divine awareness form the focus of a principle which is to apply to every part of life. Here is the plain scriptural principle that membership of the disciplined people of God is an essential part of the Christian life (I Peter 2:5-10).

Furthermore, the sacramental principle that God declares the spiritual through the natural involves that the visible form of the church is not a matter of spiritual indifference (Eph. 3:1-12). It is not enough for Christians to *say* that they are all one loving body in Christ. Their church life must show it (James 2:1-5). Their discipline must be such as to exemplify their loving cohesive unity in outward and convincing form to the world. The organization, in the sense of officials, committees, power-structure, buildings, and budgets, may change and change again. The organism of spiritual *discipline* should convincingly and practically display the church's unity of every time and place in Christ. Our unevangelical failure is that in the church we so often have an abundance of organization, yet lack discipline.

The phrase "religionless Christianity" has attracted attention in some theological quarters. It was coined by a great

Christian, Dietrich Bonhoeffer, though he would doubtless have been astonished at what some of his disciples have made of it! We are not concerned with what he may have meant by the phrase, but with what the unevangelicals commonly mean now. They generally appear to intend that in the secular age the church will largely die out as a visible, disciplined, worshiping body committed to a specific belief in God's saving work in the divine Son. Christianity will continue simply as a tradition of certain humane values embodying "the spirit of Jesus," diffused and operative in the general body of secular society. The evangelical (and the Catholic) must insist that anything of this sort is a total sellout of Christian faith, and cannot be regarded as a reinterpretation of the Christian faith in the forms of a new age. The fatal flaw is that this envisages that the day will come when man will no longer be found *worshiping*. He will no longer hold as the focus of his life personal communion with the living God of the Bible. We candidly admit that growing millions of people are in just this religionless condition, but we cannot admit that this is anything but a monstrously unnatural and unhealthy condition for man. For man to be content to remain unaware of God is the sleep of his noblest and most humane faculties. What is often called the "death of God" is in fact the death of man!

Prayer

The evangelical must insist upon the validity of intercessory prayer, including prayer that involves God's providential oversight of the order of nature (Matt. 6:9-13, 7:7-12; Luke 18:1; James 5:16). It is certainly more important to pray for growth in grace and for the spread of the Gospel than for health or good fortune, but the argument that spiritual blessings are the only subjects of intelligent prayer answers to the naturalistic idea that the physical world is a determined system. We should only pray for the nonphysical. This limitation upon prayer in fact implies that prayer is merely a psychological means of autosuggestion and mass suggestion by which a man can manipulate himself to "feel different," though nothing is in fact made any different.

Belief in the reasonableness of intercessory prayer is a leading touchstone of belief in the active, loving, personal, living God of the Bible (Psalm 145:9-19). We do not suppose that by intercession we can make God change his mind, and so bend the plan for the government of the universe. Yet God is interested (Matt. 6:7-8, 10:29-31), and can work blessing through the working of that universal law. The mark of fully Christian prayer, however, is "if it be thy will" (Luke 22:42). This is not an escape clause, so that one can argue if one's prayer is apparently not answered that one has not in fact prayed. It is a token that the purpose of prayer is that man may be so guided and enlightened as to become the fully cooperative instrument of God in the accomplishment of his all-wise and good purpose, which includes the blessing of the man of prayer (II Cor. 12:7-9).

The case in point is prayer for the sick. The evangelical believer will certainly follow the command of scripture and pray for the recovery of the sick (James 5:14-15). He will pray believingly, knowing that God possesses many mysterious resources of healing. Yet the Christian as he prays knows that the prayer for healing is bound to be denied in the end, because it is part of the will of a good and loving God for his children that this life should come to an end (Phil. 1:21-24). Thus it is not lack of faith in prayer for the sick to say "if it be thy will," for we do not know how long it is good for our loved ones, or for ourselves, to live. We only know that it would not be good for them or for us to live in this world forever (Pss. 73:23-26, 90:10, 12).

The Sacraments

The great evangelicals such as Luther, Calvin, and the Wesleys all held exalted views of the meaning and importance of the sacraments of Baptism and Holy Communion. A revival of sacramental devotion is the rightful and God-appointed partner to a revival of powerful evangelical preaching. Nor is there anything false to the gospel of salvation by grace through faith in the profession of a clear and strong doctrine of the sacraments, which the informed evangelical will confidently affirm to be scriptural.

Holy Baptism

The evangelical needs to reaffirm the New Testament teaching that baptism is the means ordained by our Lord for union with the church, which can and ought to be the means of a gift of the indwelling Spirit, and a decisive beginning to the Christian life (John 3:5; Acts 2:37-41, 22:12-16; Rom. 6:3-6). If the evangelical cannot honestly accept that God performs this spiritual change in response to the prayers of the church for the child of Christian parents, and in a manner suited to the spiritual development of a child, then he ought to restrict baptism to adult believers who are consciously converted. What ought *not* to be done is to make the worst of both worlds and allow this sacrament to sink down in the estimation of the people until it becomes no more than an occasion for thanking God for the baby and promising to bring him up as a Christian.

Holy Communion

The mature evangelical will certainly seek to teach adequate New Testament views regarding the sacramental life of the church. To set apart the bread and wine by saying over them our Lord's solemn words, with a sincere intention of obeying our Lord's command, and then in faith to eat and to drink (I Cor. 11:23-27) are the means ordained by God whereby the church on earth makes herself one with Christ the Great High Priest as he offers his sacrifice in heaven (Heb. 9:11-14, 13:10). A special realization of Christ's presence with the church is guaranteed to those who do this (Luke 24:35). Holy Communion, then, is the means whereby the church takes for herself her share of that which Christ accomplished for the world in his death and resurrection (I Cor. 10:15-16). Holy Communion is the characteristic act of Christian worship and the mark of union in the church (Acts 2:41-42; I Cor. 10:17, 11:18-22). It is to be united with the preaching of the word, to which it is the fitting climax (Acts 20:7-11). The incarnational and sacramental principle that runs through all God's spiritual dealings with man—that he gives the inward and spiritual through the natural and outward—comes to its climax of Christian experience in these sacramental high points of the life of the church.

QUESTIONS

1. Ought the church to express its unity in its outward discipline and ministry, or is it sufficient for it to profess the same message, though organized separately?

2. Is it really possible for very diverse social, economic, national, or racial groups to cooperate harmoniously in the same congregation? or is it wiser to settle for separate churches?

3. What does history show about the spiritual wisdom of

a group's leaving the old easygoing church to form a new strict congregation?

4. Have the great revivals of the past started inside or outside the church of the times? What do you think is the prospect for the future?

5. Is it right to pray for success in an examination? for fine weather in harvest? that one's son be kept safe on military service? for victory in battle?

6. What are the pros and cons of allowing young children to partake of the Lord's Supper?

7. Is attendance at Holy Communion as valid a public confession of committal to Christ as profession of a public "conversion"? Ought it to be?

8. Jesus said of his church, "the gates of hell shall not prevail against it." Has this promise been kept?

9. In your experience, is the church held together chiefly by social forces? or religious?

VII   The Last Things

There is perhaps no subject upon which evangelicals have more unfortunately disputed among themselves, and to the diversion of Christian energy away from the main task, than our Lord's Second Advent. It is most necessary, therefore, for the evangelical of today to make a renewed and thoughtful witness, which shall be alike clear, forthright, balanced, and sober. The key to a wise judgment is surely to follow the mind of our Lord, who plainly taught the advent hope, yet without falling into the disproportion and crudity which have been associated with some types of "adventism."

We may summarize the teaching of Jesus briefly as follows: (1) Jesus' coming into the world had brought the coming of the kingdom of God, i.e., the in-breaking of the sovereign rule of God upon this world (Mark 1:15; Luke 7:19-23, 11:15-22, 17:21). (2) All men and women therefore even now live at the crisis of the ages, under the judgment of God, and in a time when every action counts eternally (Matt. 24:37-51; Mark 13:32-37). (3) However, though the Kingdom has come, it has not come in its full climax. A true but small beginning has been made, which is the promise of the fulness that shall dominate all the affairs of men (Mark 4:30-32). (4) In consequence, our Lord, the Messiah or Christ whose coming brings the Kingdom, will come again. He will come not as now, in humility to be rejected by the world and to suffer, but in open glory as the Master of the world and the Judge of all men. His coming will bring the climax of divine judgment (Matt. 24:26-30, 25:31-32; Mark 8:38; Luke 17:24). (5) The coming in glory, though certain, may be long delayed (Luke 12:35-46). Therefore the wise disciple will not occupy his mind unduly with unprofitable speculation about the precise time and manner of the coming in glory, which is not for man to know (Matt. 24:3-6, 16:1-4, Mark 13:32; Acts 1:7). Rather will he live all his days in a spirit of discipline and vigilance, as one under the judgment of God. A balanced and scriptural evangelicalism will teach a solemn expectancy of the advent hope, but with avoidance of attempts to calculate the time and to dogmatize about the precise manner.

A book of this character does not have space adequately to discuss the enigmatic text Matt. 10:23 (cf. 24:34), upon which the critics have built an immense structure of speculative thought. They have argued from it that Jesus was an adventist dreamer, who mistakenly thought that he was to come again in glory at a very early date. This notion would seem to be totally inconsistent with any faith in Christ as a divine Savior and the supreme revealer of God.

To this writer, a much more reasonable speculation to account for this undoubted obscurity in the gospel narrative is that the disciples, their minds obstinately full of Jewish dreams of an earthly kingdom (Acts 1:6), to some extent misunderstood the teaching of Jesus. The end of the age is clearly something which happens outside our historical experience, and can only be expressed in imaginative or symbolical language. However, this emphatically does not involve that this part of the faith is unimportant, or that it lacks the certainty of faith. It is simply that this nonliteral form of language is appropriate in scripture for the expression of this part of the faith. To affirm that the details of symbolism in the books of the Bible which teach the advent hope are not to be taken literally is not a sign that one is failing to take scripture seriously. The prudent evangelical does not regard himself as committed to take literally all the language of the Revelation of John. Yet he does take this book very seriously as the revelation from God of the facts of human destiny. This balance of scripture exposition needs to be kept if the preaching of the Christian hope is to be robust and convincing.

The essential truth symbolized in advent doctrine is that history will end in a manner worthy of God. Clearly this can only happen by a marvelous, saving, divine intervention in history. The only alternative ground of hope is that desperately entertained by the secular humanists, namely, the notion of the perfectibility of the human race. This doctrine holds that the human race will gradually learn by experience to become more and more moral, and so, by a long evolutionary development, will gradually save itself into the ideal human order. Clearly, in light of the bitter experience of history, there is not the slightest prospect of this happening.

The dreadful fact is that as the experience of the race advances, and human knowledge and power grow, human moral understanding develops—and so does human wickedness. Thus science has produced wonderful advances in medicine and hygiene, so that hundreds of millions are healthier than ever before. Yet we are suddenly confronted with a surprising pollution of the environment, also through science, which is coming to its grim climax in the possibility of the poisoning of the race through nuclear fallout. So we are both more healthy, and less healthy!

Mass communication has made possible the dream of a society in which not just the few, but everyone may enjoy a life of culture. Yet the same media in the hands of commerce have lifted the idle gossip, the cynical slander, the smutty yarn, and the suggestive drawing from their ancient furtive position into multimillion-dollar industries, which strive with diabolical psychological skill to overthrow all the values which the educators try to lift up. So we are both in one way more civilized than of old, and in another less!

There has been a quickening of international conscience, and the "advanced" nations, at least to some extent, give assistance to the undeveloped, instead of enslaving them as they have done time immemorial. Yet never before were the relations between the nations more obviously adjusted on the basis of a balance of sheer terror.

Thus, on the one hand, we may see the authentic operation of the Spirit of God in history, working a clearer realization of moral good. Yet, at the same time, and in the same process, evil is showing itself to be ever more diabolically evil. This truth is pronounced by our Lord in the parable of the wheat and tares. In the long development of the world evil and good grow together, each gradually showing itself more plainly to be what it is, until the harvest (Matt. 13:24-30).

There is no hope of escape from this situation except by God's marvelous saving work. A vital part of the Christian faith, revealed particularly in the apocalyptical parts of scripture, is that God has resources which will not allow the development of ruin to go to the point of finally frustrating his good purposes in creating the world. When good has finally shown itself to be good, and evil to be evil, there will then come the "harvest." This will be the end of time, when God will cut off the process, destroy the power of evil, and show himself to be God indeed by vindicating the long-distressed cause of right. Thus in the mysterious future, history will end in a manner worthy of God. This vital hope alone enables the Christian to go on believing in the entire worthwhileness of right and good here and now, even though mankind can never reasonably hope to see satisfaction in this Age (Rev. 6:9-11).

We may now consider a restatement of the various scriptural doctrines connected with the Christian hope.

The Second Advent

The New Testament word commonly translated "coming" or "advent" is *parousia* (Matt. 24:3, 27; I Cor. 15:23; I Thess. 2:19, 4:15; James 5:7; II Pet. 3:4). *Parousia* means "royal presence." The sovereignty of a king extends at all times over all his dominions, but when he comes on a royal visit that sovereignty is realized in a special and personal way. God is the great King of all worlds at all times (Ps. 145:10-13), but when he entered the history of this world in the person of the divine Son-made-man his sovereignty was realized in a special and personal way.

The first Advent was a coming in great humility. Jesus was born as the Babe of Bethlehem, a figure of no importance to the secular society of his day. Hence he barely appears in the secular history of the time. His calling was to live a life of rejection and suffering, and so come to His victory (Matt. 8:20; Luke 24:26). The picture is of a self-satisfied world which would live its own life in its own "secular" way, snapping its fingers at God (Ps. 73:2-11). However, when God brings the history of this world to its destined end, an end worthy of himself, and shows himself to be God, he will do so by unveiling in this world the royal presence of Christ, no longer in humility, but in glory. This will occasion the climax of the coming of the Kingdom (Rev. 1:7). Christ will then be revealed as the absolute Master of the situation. All men and women, even the most proud and unwilling, will be compelled to confront him.

The evangelical will seek to make it plain that the use of the symbolical word Advent, or "Coming" does not indicate that Christ has to move from one place to another. He is a spiritual being who does not exist in a place. He is now immediately present to every soul that holds communion with him (Matt. 18:20, 28:20), though our devotional fellowship is at best a very partial realization (I Cor. 13:12). So the Lord is with the world now, though unrecognized (Rev. 3:20). The Second Coming in glory means that he who is now here, but ignored, will make his Presence known openly. One does not insist that the imaginative language such as "coming upon the clouds," etc., must of necessity be taken literally (Mark 13:26, 14:62). The Bible rightly understood, does not, we feel, answer questions such as whether Christ will make his Presence known in a "Galilean-like" shape, or how that figure could be seen in every part of the world. There is no answer to speculative questions like that. What is sufficient for faith is the revealed knowledge that his Presence will be made known personally, universally, and majestically. His Presence must be at least as majestic and as personal as was that of the Risen Christ (Acts 1:11). We must be content to let the manner remain a mystery.

The Last Judgment

It is clear that the unveiling of the Presence of Christ in glory will bring the final and open divine judgment upon all men. There is indeed a present judgment. Those who are confronted by Christ and respond to him are even now accepted by God. Those who are confronted and refuse him have already set their feet on the road to separation from God (John 3:17-21). They are self-condemned.

However, this present divine judgment is a secret judgment and, in a sense, an obscure judgment (Matt. 3:1; Rom. 14:13; I Cor. 4:5). Many men and women pass through this life apparently unconfronted with the claims of Christ, or doubtfully confronted. It is beyond our knowledge to say with certainty in what sense these are judged. The Bible is chiefly concerned with the practical issue of those who are pointedly confronted by Christ, not by this speculative problem. Furthermore, those who accept and follow Christ are in this world commonly the despised and misjudged disciples of a rejected Lord (Luke 6:26; I Cor. 4:10-13). Their merits are not commonly recognized by the men of this world, who hold vitiated standards. Conversely those who are condemned by Christ's judgment are in this world very frequently the self-confident recipients of praise, popularity, and success (Ps. 73:3-10). Finally, the present judgment is a provisional one. Those who have accepted Christ have yet by grace to persevere to the end and attain to the crown of life (I Cor. 9:27, 10:12). Those who are obstinate or unawakened may yet repent (Ezek. 33:10-11; I Tim. 1:12-15). Yet it is clear that the continuing process of judgment moves naturally to a climax. In God's day the judgment which is now often obscure will be manifest, that which is now unacknowledged will be vindicated, that which is provisional will then be final. In light of the open glory of Christ the Judge, every man and his works will be shown up for what they really are, eternally (Matt. 25:34-36, 42-43; Mark 8:38; Rev. 14:14-16, 20:4).

Eternal Life and Resurrection

The Bible employs these two terms to express the fulness of life in Christ. They come from different backgrounds: *resurrection* answering to the mind of Hebrew Christianity, *eternal life* more to the Greek mind in the early church. Nevertheless, although they reflect different interests, they are not opposites, but express complementary values in the truth of God.

The idea of resurrection answers to the Hebrew conception of man, in which the material part (the body) and the invisible and animating part (the soul or spirit) were thought of as indivisible. This is an idea quite in keeping with the attitude of modern science, which sees the invisible man (the personality) as something that matures with and acts through the developing nervous system of the body, with the material and nonmaterial parts of the human organism greatly influencing one another. In this Hebrew way of thinking, the survival of a nonmaterial "soul" without the body would not be seen as the triumph of man over death, but as the survival of a mere ghost. In the day of God the body also, that is, the whole man, is to triumph over death (Dan. 12:2).

In well-considered Christian theology the scriptural doctrine of the "resurrection of the body" does not mean that the *material* body will be reassembled in the day of Christ's glory, but that those who then belong to him will be fully alive in every faculty of human nature. They will not be ghosts, or reduced unexpressive shades of their former selves.

In the heavenly Kingdom there will be a mode of expression for the spirit of man comparable to that now provided by the physical body, but adapted for the state of glory (I Cor. 15:35-54). *216 736*

Eternal life means the "life of the heavenly sphere," life in fellowship with God (Matt. 19:16; John 3:16, 17:3; Rom. 6:23; I John 5:11). The emphasis is that it is a present gift to those who belong to Christ, and is of such quality that it cannot be broken off by the death of the physical body (John 10:28; II Cor. 4:16-18). Thus eternal life symbolizes the scriptural faith that the departed are not in a state of suspended animation awaiting a future resurrection (Luke 23:43). They are spiritually alive, with exalted powers. (Heb. 12:22-24). They are now in fellowship with God and with one another (Rev. 7:13-17, 14:13), and feel a personal interest in those who are still in this life. All this is expressed in the phrase "the communion of saints." The two beliefs, resurrection and eternal life, are certainly not inconsistent with one another, for we may believe that those who now in heaven possess eternal life are not static in that condition. As they grow "from glory to glory" (II Cor. 3:18) there may well be room for an advance in fulness of life at the resurrection.

The Millennial Kingdom

The expectation of Christ's reign on earth with his saints symbolizes the profound idea that this world, which has seen so much sin and wrong, is not destined to be "cast as rubbish to the void." It is fundamental to the Christian faith that God created the material universe for a spiritual purpose. This purpose is destined to be fulfilled, and therefore the creation is to be saved and restored (Rom. 8:19-22). It does not follow from this that the symbolical language of such a passage as Revelation 20:1-5 is necessarily to be pressed in a literal sense, as though the Millennial Kingdom were to last for a space of astronomical time, and that we are to inquire whether the period is to be "before" or "after" other of these mysterious events.

Heaven and Hell

The chief interest of evangelical faith is to affirm that the reward of good is not pleasure dispensed by God, and that the recompense for evil is not torture applied by God. This rendering of the symbolism of the Bible leads to a very superficial and unspiritual sense. In any case, the Christian is the disciple of a crucified Lord, who suffered precisely because he was altogether good. This is a standing warning against the notion of divine government by rewards and punishments.

The dreadful effect of hardening one's heart to good is to make it more difficult to see what is good, and more difficult to do it (Isa. 6:9-10; John 3:19-20; I Tim. 4:1-2). Thus in trifling with Christ and his claims one faces the inherent danger of hardening one's heart to a point of no return (Matt. 26:24; Luke 16:26). This is the final recompense of evil. It is not that at a certain point God withdraws his love and issues his eternal vengeance. This sort of hell would indeed be inconsistent with the nature of a God of universal love. The dreadful recompense is that man can so harden himself by calling good his evil, and evil his good, that the more he is pursued by the love of God, the more he runs away. To find too late that one has made oneself into a being like this, in a universe ruled by the sovereign God of holy love, is final perdition (Rev. 6:15-17). This is not an external penalty of suffering visited by a God of justice who has ceased to forgive. The immeasurable spiritual woe of hell is the natural and fitting end of the process of seeking in pride and rebellion to live in God's world in a way otherwise than God in his goodness has provided.

Similarly, the great reward (if such it may be called) of good is good (Matt. 13:12). Those who open their hearts to the good and do good find in themselves an increased power both to see the good for what it is and to do it, and also an increased joy in the doing of it (Rev. 7:15-17, 22:3-5). The natural and fitting end of the process is to be wholly and finally confirmed in good. This is heaven. Thus the highest good is the vision of God (I John 3:2).

QUESTIONS

1. Ought the Christian to be more worried than other people about the condition of the world, or less?

2. Is it possible to vindicate God's government of the world as just apart from a life beyond the grave, and a last judgment?

3. We sing the hymn "Rise up, O men of God!" which speaks of bringing in "the day of brotherhood" and ending "the night of wrong." What relation has this to our Lord's gospel of the Kingdom?

4. Would Christian theology do better to speak of the survival of the soul rather than the resurrection of the body? Can we speak of both?

5. We sing:

> Lo, he comes with clouds descending,
>   Once for favored sinners slain;
> Thousand thousand saints attending,

> Swell the triumph of his train;
> Hallelujah! Hallelujah!
> God appears on earth to reign.

Does language of this sort quicken your blood, nerve your courage, and confirm your faith, or does it "turn you off"? Why should language of this sort be more widely appreciated than it was before 1914?

6. Milton writes in *Paradise Lost*:

> The mind is its own place, and in itself
> Can make a heaven of hell, a hell of heaven.

Is this a sufficient account of heaven and hell?

7. Is a completely good God absolutely *bound* to forgive everyone in the end, no matter what?

8. Would it be consistent with the goodness of God to annihilate the finally impenitent? If so, ought he to have done it long ago?

Annotated Bibliography

Thousands of books, of every degree of detail and difficulty, are available for reading. For the purpose of this publication we have limited ourselves to listing a few that we have come across which are fairly easy to read, and which should be generally accessible. We have not included denominational handbooks. We have included some books that contain useful bibliographies of further and more advanced reading.

I am grateful to my friend, the Reverend Theodore Williams, one of our graduate students, for invaluable help in compiling this bibliography.

Barclay, William. *The Apostles' Creed for Everyman.* New York: Harper & Row, 1967.

A straightforward outline of basic Christian doctrine, from the point of view of an outstanding New Testament scholar.

Bruce, Frederich F. *New Testament Documents: Are They Reliable?* Grand Rapids: Eerdmans Publishing Company, 1943.

An able and informed defense of the foundations of Christian belief.

Lawson, John. *Comprehensive Handbook of Christian Doctrine*. Englewood Cliffs, N. J.: Prentice-Hall, 1967.

A much fuller outline of Christian doctrine than is possible in this small book, dealing in more detail with a wider variety of issues, though so far as possible in nontechnical language.

Lewis, Clive S. *Mere Christianity*. New York: The Macmillan Company, 1952.

A classic defense of Christian belief and morals written in characteristic and engaging literary style by a prominent intellectual unbeliever converted to the Christian faith.

———. *The Screwtape Letters*. New York: The Macmillan Company, 1943.

A whimsical essay on the subject of evil. There are also many other books, mostly short and easy to read, by this excellent writer.

Phillips, J. B. *Ring of Truth*. New York: The Macmillan Company, 1967.

A passionate and eloquent defense of Christian faith from a scholar who has spent his life with the New Testament.

Ramsey, A. Michael. *The Resurrection of Christ*. Philadelphia: The Westminster Press, 1946.

An authoritative little book by the scholarly Archbishop of Canterbury on this central point of the Christian faith.

Rupp, E. Gordon. *Last Things First*. Philadelphia: Fortress Press, 1964.

Written in characteristic humane and humorous style on Christian fellowship and forgiveness, and the resurrection to eternal life.

Sangster, William E. *The Path to Perfection*. Nashville: Abingdon-Cokesbury, 1943.

A scholarly work on Christian holiness by a saint, and one of the outstanding evangelical preachers of our day.

Starkey, Lycurgus. *The Holy Spirit at Work in the Church*. Nashville: Abingdon Press, 1965.

An evangelical treatment of the work of the Holy Spirit in the church, and in personal religious experience.

Stott, John R. W. *Basic Christianity*. Grand Rapids: Eerdmans Publishing Company, 1957.

A good outline of the system of Christian theology for beginners.

Whale, John S. *Christian Doctrine*. New York: The Macmillan Company, 1941.

A short outline of Christian theology, clear and uncompromising in evangelical outlook, and scholarly in treatment, basing itself on scripture, the writers of the ancient church, and the great Protestant reformers.

Williams, Charles. *The Descent of the Dove*. New York: Meridian Books, Grand Rapids: Eerdmans Publishing Company, 1956.

A treatment in unconventional style of the development of Christian devotion and thought down the centuries under the renewing guidance of the Holy Spirit.

WITHDRAWN